ONE
SPLIT
SECOND

The Distracted Driving Epidemic
How It Kills and How We Can Fix It

Vijay Dixit
with
Antonia Felix

Wisdom
Editions

Minneapolis

Wisdom
Editions

Minneapolis

FIRST EDITION MARCH 2016

ONE SPLIT SECOND: *The Distracted Driving Epidemic: How It Kills and How We Can Fix It*

For information, write to Calumet Editions, 8422 Rosewood Drive, Chanhassen, MN 55317

Figures 4, 5, and 6 reprinted, by permission, from "Measuring Cognitive Distraction in the Automobile," "Measuring Cognitive Distraction in the Automobile II," and Measuring Cognitive Distraction in the Automobile III." © 2013, 2014, 2015 AAA Foundation for Traffic Safety.

Figure 7 reprinted, by permission, from Jason Chein et al, "Peers Increase Adolescent Risk Taking by Enhancing Activity in the Brain's Reward Circuitry," p. F5. © 2010 by Blackwell Publishing.

Figure 8 reprinted, by permission, from Janet I. Creaser et al, "Are Cellular Phone Blocking Applications Effective for Novice Teen Drivers?", p. 79. © 2015 by Elsevier Ltd. and National Safety Council.

Printed in the United States of America.

10 9 8 7 6 5 4 3 2 1

Cover and interior design: Gary Lindberg

ISBN: 978-1-939548-44-3

ONE
SPLIT
SECOND

The Distracted Driving Epidemic
How It Kills and How We Can Fix It

Vijay Dixit
with
Antonia Felix

For Shreya, whose loss became the inspiration
for this book.

Contents

Acknowledgements

I extend my heart-filled thanks to all my friends and loved ones who joined me in my journey of writing this book. My deepest thanks go to my very dear daughter Shreya, or Tultul, as I lovingly called her. She inspired and infused me from the astral space with a unique form of energy that kept me composed and focused while still carrying the heavy burden of her loss. I could not have done it without that scaffolding.

I knew that writing this book would be a challenging task and require expert resources. Thanks to Gary Lindberg, my publisher and friend who introduced me to Antonia Felix, the accomplished author who helped me communicate complex ideas in a very simple language. Thank you, Antonia.

I owe dual thanks to former Minnesota Secretary of State Mark Ritchie and his wife, Nancy. Not only have they partnered in our quest for building distraction-free driver communities, but willingly shared their story of losing their daughter Rachel to an impaired driver fourteen years ago.

A large number of safety advocates, educators, and law enforcement personnel became valued information sources. Among them are Deborah Hersman, CEO, National Safety Council; Commissioner Demona Dohman, Donna Burger, Col. Matt Langer and Tiffani Schweigart of the Minnesota Department of Public Safety; Paul Aaasan, President, and Lisa Kons of the Minnesota Safety Council; Nancy Johnson, Co-Founder, Minnesotans for Safe Driving; Gordy Pehrson and Hal Campbell of the Minnesota Office of Traffic Safety; Nichole Morris of the HumanFirst Program at the University of Minnesota; Jake Nelson of AAA Foundation; David Strayer of the University of Utah; Matt Richtel of the *New York Times*; Attorneys Robert Speeter and Art Kosieradzki; Frank Douma of the University of Minnesota; and Susan Reynolds. They each deserve special thanks.

Thank you Jacy Good, Joel Feldman, and Jennifer Zamora-Jameson for sharing stories of your losses and advocacy work.

With deep gratitude, I also give thanks to Sharon Driscoll-Gehrman and Jon Cummings of Minnesotans for Safe Driving for uplifting the family at our time of extreme grief. Almost nine years later, both Sharon and Jon are still there, helping us in all our initiatives, including this book.

I would like to thank former U.S. Secretary of Transportation Ray LaHood for making himself available to discuss the problem with us, and for offering his valuable insights for inclusion in the book.

I offer my special gratitude to Senator Amy Klobuchar for agreeing to talk to us about legislative headwinds and educational funding challenges for distracted driving programs. I sincerely appreciate her support of our foundation activities, including the establishment of Distraction-free Driving Clubs in high schools, and for writing the Foreword to the book.

Thanks go out to my dear friend Ram Ramabhadran, who was always willing and able to recharge my thinking with frequent brainstorming sessions.

I cannot forget three of Shreya's best friends: Bridget from BSM High School, Kristen from Bryant College, and Barbara from the Bel Canto Choir. Thank you for sharing your Shreya memories for the book.

Lastly, I would like to thank my lovely wife Rekha, my loving daughter Nayha, and my dear son-in-law David for their unending supply of much-needed moral and emotional support. All three helped me sustain a high confidence level throughout this book project. I love you.

Despite my sincere effort to acknowledge all who helped me in transforming my thoughts into words, I am bound to forget some, and for that I ask forgiveness.

About the Authors

VIJAY DIXIT is a management and business process design consultant who has worked in the IT, health insurance, and energy industries. A graduate of the Indian Institute of Technology, he moved to the U.S. in 1974 to do graduate work in clean technologies and business management.

After losing their daughter Shreya to a distracted driver in 2007, Vijay and his wife Rekha established the Shreya R. Dixit Memorial Foundation to conduct awareness and education campaigns in the states of Minnesota and Connecticut. In addition to his advocacy work with the foundation, Vijay drew on his engineering background to pioneer the development of the world's first Adaptive Massive Open Online Course (aMOOC) for combating distracted driving. Vijay and Rekha live in Eden Prairie, Minnesota.

ANTONIA FELIX is the *New York Times* bestselling author of sixteen nonfiction books, including several political biographies, most recently *Sonia Sotomayor: The True American Dream*, (Berkley/Penguin USA). She is also the author of two novels, a play, and short fiction. Antonia is an adjunct instructor at Hamline University and lives with her husband on a ranch outside St. Paul, Minnesota.

Engage with us at:

OneSplitSecondBook.com

Foreword

Vijay Dixit's book is an important contribution toward raising awareness about the dangers of distracted driving. For the Dixit family, the issue is personal. Vijay lost his daughter, Shreya, to a distracted driver on November 1, 2007. She was only 19 years old. Such tragedy would sideline many, but Vijay pushed forward and made it his life's mission to end distracted driving and prevent other families from going through what his family has endured.

Drawing on the expertise from those in the field, including safety professionals and researchers, the latest facts and figures, and personal stories, Vijay has created a comprehensive guide to distracted driving and potential solutions. He explores how technology, education, and laws can change our behavior and improve safety. He offers an original framework for student-led, distraction-free-driving advocacy clubs in high schools to help teens learn responsible driving behaviors. I commend Vijay for launching clubs in three Minnesota high schools in 2015 and setting them up to achieve measurable goals.

Over the years I have met with families across the country—including the Dixits—who have lost loved ones when a driver took his or her eyes off the road. Their heartbreaking stories remind us that distracted driving is a matter of life and death. Whether it is texting with a friend, searching for music files, or typing directions into the GPS, distracted driving is putting drivers, passengers, and pedestrians at risk. It only takes a moment of distracted driving to cause a tragedy. Five seconds is the average time a driver's eyes are off the road while texting. For a driver traveling at 55 miles per hour, that's like covering the length of a football field blindfolded.

No text message is worth dying for.

In the age of smartphones, distracted driving is playing an outsized role and endangering everyone on the road. Every day, nine people are killed and more than 1,100 people are injured in the United States in crashes involving distracted driving. Nearly half of all U.S. high school students aged 16 or older admitted to texting or emailing while behind the wheel.[1]

More must be done to quell this epidemic that is sweeping the country. That is why I worked with U.S. Senators John Hoeven (R-ND), Cory Booker (D-NJ), and Lisa Murkowski (R-AK) to introduce bipartisan legislation to crack down on distracted driving in Minnesota and across the country. In 2014, millions of dollars in federal grant money that was designated to reduce distracted driving went unused because of overly stringent qualifications. Our bipartisan legislation would make it easier for states that are taking steps to curb distracted driving to qualify for these federal grants to support their efforts.

We've pushed this legislation for years, and finally our hard work has paid off. Our legislation was included in the long-term, bipartisan transportation bill—the Fixing America's Surface Transportation (FAST) Act—that Congress passed and the President signed into law on December 3, 2015.

The FAST Act moves us ahead by investing in our infrastructure, creating jobs, and improving safety. It only happened because many people—from different backgrounds and political beliefs—were willing to work together to get it done. This is also what it will take to make distracted driving as taboo as drunk driving. We need to join forces to let every current and future driver know that someone who texts and drives is just as impaired as someone who drinks and drives.

I believe that drivers of all ages, especially parents, teenagers, teachers, school administrators, driving instructors, and agency officials, will benefit from this book. The title, *One Split Second*, says it all: Our lives can be changed forever or lost in the blink of an eye if we drive distracted.

I am proud to know Vijay, his family, and those who support his foundation. This book is a call to action, written with heart.

U.S. Senator Amy Klobuchar
Minneapolis, Minnesota
January 28, 2016

Author's Note

The seed for this book was planted by a traumatic tragedy on November 1, 2007. It all happened on a highway that connects Madison, Wisconsin, with the Twin Cities of Minneapolis/Saint Paul, Minnesota. On that day the driver of a car in which my daughter Shreya was riding got distracted and caused a crash, killing Shreya on the spot.

This book, however, does not dwell on that loss. Instead, it focuses on the most critical issues surrounding distraction, some controversial and many, I believe, thought provoking. These issues include how technology, laws, and education can help fight driver distraction. Despite its tragic beginning, the eight-year-long journey since that fateful day has taken me on a path that psychologists call 'post traumatic growth.' Recent studies tell us that trauma can also produce specific psychological benefits. In the wake of traumatic experiences, people may evolve out of their brokenness and report positive changes. This book describes a product of that post-traumatic growth, our efforts to tackle a problem that has become an epidemic among drivers of all ages.

The unique experience gained while writing this book has been very therapeutic for me. It has given me the opportunity to transform a negative situation into something positive that may help others cope with similar circumstances. I hope to move forward with many of the new ideas I have discovered, using them to shape new initiatives at the Shreya R. Dixit Memorial Foundation, the organization my family established to help build distraction-free-driver communities.

Your interest in this book shows that you care about the safety of your loved ones and everyone else who shares the road. It also reveals that you want to be part of the solution to end the distracted driving epidemic, and for that I am deeply grateful.

Vijay Dixit
Eden Prairie, Minnesota
February 22, 2016

PART 1

Moments of Truth

Vijay Dixit & Antonia Felix

Chapter 1

Paradise Lost

Without you, the ground thaws,
the rain falls, the grass grows.
Without you, the seeds root,
the flowers bloom, the children play.
The stars gleam, the poets dream,
the eagles fly, without you.
The earth turns, the sun burns,
but I die, without you.

—from *Rent* (the musical)
by Jonathan Larson

It was going to be a very special weekend.

In the first days of November, 2007, both of our daughters were coming home to Eden Prairie, Minnesota, to celebrate Diwali, the biggest festival of the year for Hindus in India, celebrated much like Christmas is in the United States. We were holding

9

the celebration a bit early that year as a kick-off to the main event—my trip with our elder daughter, Nayha, 25, who lived in Atlanta. A few days after our family weekend, Nayha was going to join me on a vacation to India to celebrate Diwali in our ancestral home for the first time. I had not experienced Diwali in India since I had left in 1974, so returning with Nayha was going to be a big adventure for both of us.

Our younger daughter, Shreya, 19, was traveling home from the University of Wisconsin (UW) in Madison, where she had just begun her sophomore year a few weeks earlier. We had not seen her since we drove down to Madison to celebrate her birthday on September 16th.

The house was decorated with lights inside and out, gifts were piled up in the living room, and my wife, Rekha, was preparing all of our daughter's favorite Indian and American dishes. Nayha's birthday, coming up on November 5th, added to the excitement and anticipation.

That Friday evening, around 6:40 p.m., Shreya called her mother to tell her that she had found a ride to Minnesota with another student who would be driving to the Twin Cities area. They would be heading out soon, and Shreya had already arranged for one of her friends to meet her when they got close to the Twin Cities and bring her home. Shreya did not know the driver well, even though they had attended the same high school in Eden Prairie. She had heard from some mutual friends that this girl was driving to Minnesota, and thought perhaps she could ride along.

Shreya liked the idea, she told her mom, because the four-and-a-half-hour drive would be faster and more comfortable than taking the bus. She did not know the two other students, girlfriends of the driver, who would be riding along. But Shreya got along well with everyone. She was, as all her friends and everyone who had ever crossed her path knew, a kind, lively and beautiful light in this world. Everyone loved Shreya.

She was coming home to celebrate Diwali with us and to wish me and her sister a wonderful journey. To Shreya, her sister was not Nayha but 'Didi,' the traditional Hindi word for an older sister. And to me, Shreya was always 'Tultul,' or butterfly.

At about 8:15 that night, while I was practicing a couple of songs I was going to sing with friends when I got to India, Rekha suddenly began to feel strange. She was trembling, and I had never seen such a bewildered look on her face. Her hands shook uncontrollably, and she said she wanted to go to bed. I had to help her up the stairs because her legs were so shaky she could hardly walk. I brought her a glass of orange juice, and after she sat on the bed for a minute I told her that she should take a shower—it would make her feel better. She did, and when she went back to bed she asked me to sing the songs I had been practicing, to help her relax.

After a few minutes of singing, Rekha seemed a little better. We decided to get some sleep before Shreya arrived with her friend. Not long after we turned out the light, the phone rang. Rekha answered it, and after listening for a few seconds she threw down the phone on the bed. "This woman says that Shreya has been in an accident!" she cried. "You must talk to her—I cannot!"

I picked up the phone and the woman said that she was the mother of the girl who was driving her friends and Shreya home, and there had been a car accident. She said the crash occurred about forty-five minutes out of Madison, and that Shreya was in the hospital in Mauston, the nearest town. A helicopter was on its way to airlift her to the University Hospital in Madison. She gave me the phone number to the hospital in Mauston, and hung up.

I called the hospital and no one picked up the phone. Then I called the driver's mother again and told her that no one had answered. "No, no," she said, "we just talked to them. They are there." I called again and that time a nurse picked up.

"This is Vijay Dixit," I said. "You have my daughter there… Shreya." The moment I mentioned her name the nurse told me to hold on. She put me on hold for what seemed like hours, until a woman doctor finally came on. She explained that they had used breathing tubes and had tried everything to revive her, but our daughter had passed away. "What do you mean she passed away?" I said. "She was nineteen!"

"I am so sorry," the doctor said, "but we could not revive her."

* * *

We learned more about the crash later on. At the hospital, we heard that the driver and two other passengers were not injured. I asked the driver, "What were you doing?"

The girl was traumatized. "I was just reaching for a napkin," she said.

Two witnesses who had been driving behind them reported that the car suddenly swerved very sharply for no reason. The road was straight as an arrow and perfectly dry, but the car jerked and drove into the grassy meridian. The driver evidently overcompensated, ran over and smashed a culvert, and then slammed the front right side of the Chevrolet Suburban into a cement pylon of the overpass. That was the only overpass in the ten-mile stretch between Mauston and New Lisbon.

The first responders quickly called for a jaws of life to cut open the car because Shreya was too badly crushed to pull out. A lot of time was lost trying to get her out of the car. When they finally got to her, she was not breathing and her blood pressure was very low. They placed her in the ambulance and inserted a breathing tube. Her blood pressure went up a little bit, but it was too late. She died in the hospital, and the UW helicopter turned around in midair and returned to Madison.

We never learned more details about the driver's distracted action that caused the crash and took Shreya's life. All we know is that she turned away to get a napkin. And in that one split second, all was lost.

The song I had been singing before the phone call, before Rekha's hands began to shake, was a message to myself... and maybe a message from Shreya. Rekha's physical reaction to the crash while it was happening was only one of the surreal experiences surrounding Shreya's passing. The words to that song, "Do Pal," which was very popular in India at the time, was another. One verse of that song speaks to a situation happening two hundred miles away—and somewhere deep in our awareness, through our bond with Shreya:

Just for a moment, for a couple of seconds
The caravan of my dreams stopped.
The caravan of my dreams stopped for two seconds.
Suddenly, I realized that
You went this way, I went that way.
You were my rose, you were my life,

14

But the moment the caravan stopped,
You went this way, I went that way.[2]

Witnesses to Love and Loss, In Their Own Words

Shreya's loss was devastating to everyone who knew her.

Kristen, her freshman-year roommate at Bryant College, had quickly become her best friend and part of the family. Without knowing it, we had lived near Kristen's family in Connecticut before moving to Minnesota, so the two girls already had some friends in common. When they unpacked that first day at school, they discovered that they had the same bedsheets, skin moisturizers, and other odd coincidences, which instantly bonded them. "We were inseparable from the first day... two peas in a pod," Kristen said. "Our birthdays were exactly a week apart, so those first two weeks of school we celebrated our birthdays. She felt like a sister to me."

They were both business majors, and Kristen recalled that Shreya did well in economics and liked the international business classes. "She talked about wanting to work for an international company. She had traveled to India with her family many times and wanted to use her Indian background, which she cherished."

After freshman year Shreya decided to transfer to the University of Wisconsin-Madison, and during her first semester there she missed Kristen very much. They had one last visit together, which Kristen will never forget:

> Our birthdays came right before she passed away, and she had told her parents that the only thing she wanted for her birthday was to visit me in Boston. She came for a week and a half. My fondest memory of that amazing trip was of riding the red line, going over Boston Harbor, and both of us crying and saying that that was our dream place to live. We promised that after college we would be roommates again in Boston.
>
> That was right before we said good-bye. I went straight to campus to take a test and she left me a voicemail. When I got home, I saw that she had left me a handmade card.
>
> She was such a shining light. And she was the most positive person I've ever met.
>
> Remembering Shreya reminds me not to get too bogged down or upset over the small things. Life's too short... live it to the fullest. That's what she always said.

* * *

Bridget, one of Shreya's best friends at Benilde-St. Margaret's High School and also a fellow student at the University of Wisconsin, recalled the impact of Shreya's death on her own life. The day before the fatal crash, Bridget had celebrated Halloween with Shreya.

"I spent a long time after that contemplating life and death, what happens after death, and the point of life," she said. "It helped me focus on how short life is and how important it is to make life meaningful while we do have it. I'm not the kind of person who thinks that everything happens for a reason, but I think you can learn something from everything that happens."

Bridget misses the lighthearted joy that Shreya brought to everything, the love she had for her friends, and their shared passion for music:

> Shreya had this infectious joy and laughter around her. When you were with Shreya you were always smiling. I miss that infectious joy. When you were with her you felt that you weren't alone and that life was good and you could get through anything.

> I found a letter she had written to me when I was going through a hard time. I found it during the week after she died. She wrote, 'Stay strong, B, you're an awesome person, you're going to get through this, you're not alone.' All these things could have been taken in the context of her death, things I needed to hear then, too. I read part of that at her funeral service. It was support from Shreya

herself, telling me how to be happy, how to get through that grieving period. That was the way she supported people. She could sense when you needed somebody, and she would be that somebody.

In high school there's a lot of drama, especially with girls. You're friends and then not friends, but Shreya was everybody's friend. She played that role in our group of friends. We are still a group, and we recently got together for a bachelorette party. I looked around and thought, what would it be like if Shreya were still with us? Would we have stayed closer? She was definitely that kind of glue. She never succumbed to the drama and ditched friends and came back to friends. She was just always there.

One of the most important things to Shreya were people and her relationships. She was really in tune with people's needs, being there for them, and being friends with them, which was rare in someone so young. She was very focused on others. And she loved music.

Her favorite thing to do was go to outdoor music concerts and festivals, and our summers revolved around them. One thing that will always remind me of Shreya is the soundtrack of *Rent*—we were both obsessed with that music. We'd drive around after school with her sunroof open and the windows down blasting *Rent* and singing along. Music seemed to sustain her. She had some hard times in her freshman year at a school out east. After she died we found a little notebook in her purse with a note to our friend Jackie. It was a list of how to survive freshman year, basically a list of all these music concerts we were going to go to.

When people ask me what Shreya meant to me, I think about what impact I am having on people. I reflect on what she did, living every moment to its fullest. Her wanting to be there for her friends and bringing joy and laughter to people—that was unique to Shreya. Her death definitely helped me grow up. It made me a better person. And thinking of the foundation her parents launched in her name, I learned so much about how you create something out of nothing.

Bridget's father, Fran, a guidance counselor at the girls' high school, remembered Shreya as a loving girl, someone who had a very positive influence on all her friends, and a teenager who was just as eager to visit with the older generations in the family as she was to be with Bridget. "She loved coming over for dinner when Bridget's grandmother and her friend, who were in their eighties, were there." After Shreya's death, Fran and his wife went to Madison with us to pick up Shreya's belongings. He recalled that the experience changed everything and turned him into an advocate for distraction-free driving. "It was really hard to watch them go through it," Fran said. "We just thought, *what if this were Bridget?*"

Fran not only changed his driving habits and stopped using his phone behind the wheel, but also brought the message to the students at Benilde-St. Margaret's High School. He began to talk to them about the risks of distracted driving and arranged for AAA and other safety organizations to present panels at the school every year. He also joined the board of the foundation.

Music was the heartbeat of Shreya's life and her friendships. She and her sister, Nayha, studied violin and classical Indian dance, Kathak, when they were children. Shreya started violin at about age three with a tiny, toy-like violin used in the Suzuki method. And from the beginning, Shreya loved to sing. She would turn on the radio and sing along to all kinds of songs. When she was just six or seven she learned to sing "Memories" from *Cats* by memory. She loved that song and by fourth grade had mastered it so beautifully that her voice instructor asked her to sing it in a class recital. In sixth grade she was chosen to sing in the Connecticut Children's Choir, a special indication of her talent, since all the other members were in high school.

After we moved to Minnesota and Shreya began junior high, she focused her music studies on singing. Her voice teacher at the MacPhail School of Music in Minneapolis, Oksana Bryn, taught her classical technique and repertoire, and Shreya loved her. Shreya had a beautiful voice and was often chosen to sing solos in her choirs.

Shreya's friend Barbara made her first connection with Shreya through music. They both sang in a Twin Cities choir called Bel Canto that traveled to Europe for a month one summer, and during that trip the two became close friends. "There's something about being able to express things through song that is powerful," Barbara said, "and it connects people. Connecting is what Shreya did so well, so singing was such a good fit for her."

Barbara remembers Shreya as an adventurous and curious spirit. "She wanted to see the world and explore and leave her mark in the world in whatever form," she said. "She talked about working in the Peace Corps in India, or working in another more impoverished country. She was interested in working with kids and families that for whatever reason were struggling, to connect with them through some type of service."

After Shreya's funeral, Barbara struggled with not knowing exactly what happened in the crash. She was heartbroken and plagued with questions—had Shreya been in pain? Did she suffer? The ambiguity tormented her. And then, mysteriously, she found peace:

> About a week after the funeral I had a dream about Shreya, and it was the most vivid dream

21

I have ever had. In the dream Shreya told me what happened at that moment. She said that she took a deep breath and let everything go, and she was OK. I woke up in tears. I believe those we have really loved and cared about have the ability to reassure us that everything is all right. We can continue with our own individual process and keep that special place for them, and also experience healing.

* * *

Later on, after we started the foundation, Barbara became an advocate, telling Shreya's story and raising awareness about distracted driving at her college. She talked about the impact that Shreya's death had on her and her friends in hopes that it would change young drivers' behavior. Today, she wishes Shreya could be moving into new parts of life with her and their close circle of friends as they get married and start their families. "I miss not being able to share those things with her," Barbara said. "I miss most seeing who she would have become."

Nayha, Shreya's "Didi"

Our daughter Nayha was six years old when Shreya was born. She was so excited to have a baby sister that she brought her to show-and-tell in first grade. "I distinctly remember someone else bringing in an eraser or a pencil or something," Nayha said, "and I brought in my sister." Nayha left for college when Shreya was twelve, so they did not spend a lot of time with each other during Shreya's teenage years. But when Shreya graduated from high school they started getting closer, like friends. Nayha came to know Shreya's happy spirit and easygoing approach to life even more in that time, and it stays with her:

> I would worry about everything. I remember when she came with me to the post office to drop off my graduate school applications and I wrote down the addresses. She said, 'You're taking forever to write down these addresses. Don't worry, it will be fine.' I spent ten minutes on them, and she said, 'It doesn't matter. You're going to either get in or not get in, and that's what it's going to be.'

> Now I try to live more like that. I try to be more of the free spirit and the person that she was. She connected with so many more people than I was able to connect with, in a deep way. I had a hard time bringing a lot of people in. I was very social when I was in high school and had a lot of friends, but as far as connecting with people on a deep level, she had an incredibly meaningful relationship with the people she knew... with Dad, with Mom. I wish we could have spent more time talking about our lives, but we weren't really at that point where we could. She was just starting to find her path.

* * *

Nayha lives in San Francisco with her husband, David, a radiation oncologist, and she herself is a medical physicist in radiation oncology. A few weeks before I finished writing this book, they announced that they were having their first child. Somewhere, we know that Shreya shares our joy in this news and will be with her Didi through this new passage of her life.

Welcome, Sorrow

After Shreya's death, Rekha and I met with one therapist after another, looking for someone to guide us through the storm. The first three simply did not work for us. Finally, we found exactly who we needed, and it was a fluke. Mentioning our frustrating search to a doctor friend one day, she stopped us short and said, "You don't need a psychiatrist, you need Susan." We made an appointment with Susan in her St. Louis Park office and from the first meeting we knew we had landed where we needed to be.

Without grief therapy, and without undergoing that therapy with Susan, our lives would be very different today. I do not believe we would be engaged with the world, have a foundation, or, for that matter, have much of a life at all. Susan began that first session by explaining that her goal as a grief therapist was to help people maintain connections with people they still need and really love, even when they are separated by death. She believes that it is crucial for people to develop a new relationship with the person who died that allows them to go on living and loving, bringing that person with them. Thanks to Susan, we learned how to bring Shreya forward with us into a new life.

Little did we know that our healing would be measured in years. The pain will never completely go away, but the chronic sorrow, as Susan called it, eventually became a normal and endurable part of life. We learned that each year holds its own challenges and transformations. Everyone goes through these phases in their own way, but in general, each year holds many common experiences for all. Year one is about survival, when those who grieve wonder if they can even make it. That was surely true for us. One of the myths about the first year of grief is that once you get to the first anniversary of the death, it will get easier. But it doesn't. It just shifts. The second year is less about survival trauma and more a period of almost unbearable missing. After that, each year has its own particular dynamics. "Dealing with a child's death is very much a five-year slog," Susan said, "and it's a lifetime of missing. But by the sixth year you have some agency in your new life." As we learned, that agency comes from creating a solid, interactive relationship with the child.

Susan provided a safe place for us to spend our trauma that first year. She simply held us in our agony. But in that process she helped us move Shreya from outside of ourselves, where we could touch, smell, and hear her, to inside ourselves. Eventually we woke up and realized we could now find Shreya inside.

Rekha and I had our own processes for making that transformation. Rekha worked with someone to deepen her meditation practice. I followed a ritual of starting each day by walking from photo to photo of Shreya in the house, saying good morning to her, and then reciting my prayers.

My Hindu prayers became a strong connecting force to Shreya. My parents lived with us when Shreya and Nayha were young, and my father taught them Hindu prayers that they would say in the morning before going to school. The girls learned them in Sanskrit, including this common one, "Tvameva mata," often spoken at the start of the day:

Tvameva mata cha pita tvameva,
Tvameva bandhu shcha sakhaa tvameva,
Tvameva vidya dravinam tvameva,
Tvameva sarvam mama deva deva.

You are my mother, You are my father,
You are my brother, You are my friend,
You are my knowledge, You are my wealth,
You are my all-in-all, O God of gods.

Reciting the prayers I had heard Shreya say helped me find an inner relationship with her. By year three I was ready to go even deeper and turn to music, one of Shreya's great loves. I began taking voice lessons with a Hindu artist, and those lessons were more of a meditation for me—I listened to her and repeated what she asked me to do with my eyes closed. I sang lullabies to the girls when they were little and have always loved to sing. The lessons helped me find a new bridge to the joy of music we shared and to form a deeper inner bond with Shreya.

We finished our regular therapy sessions with Susan about six years after Shreya's death, but we still needed to check back in on certain days that Susan called marker days. Shreya's birthday, college graduation season, and weddings of Shreya's friends were very tough on us. We learned that marker days and the five-year anniversaries of the death are the hardest. "Years one, two, and three are excruciating," Susan said. "Year four is a little more manageable, five is very hard, and six is a little more manageable again. And ten is very hard again... the anniversary date. Something about those five-year intervals is shocking."

We also learned that most who grieve reach a critical point at the end of the second year. That is when people have to make a decision as to whether they are going to exist for the rest of their years or begin to live. Thanks to Susan's help, Rekha and I each found a way to begin living again. Rekha found ways to express her love, such as reaching out to others who had lost a child. She also cooked enormous feasts at our local Hindu temple on the anniversary of Shreya's death, making food for four hundred people all by herself. Rekha was already a deeply loving person, but in some ways that quality became more powerful because it came hard earned. It is very difficult to allow your heart to feel love again after it's been broken, and she accomplished that. My path was more public and community oriented, focused on creating a foundation in Shreya's name to raise awareness about distracted driving.

Susan introduced us to a beautiful book that expresses the forward-moving process of healing after grief, Barbara Kingsolver's collection of essays called *High Tide in Tucson*. In the first essay, she writes about our instinct to keep going after traumatic loss or change:

> We hold fast to the old passions of endurance that buckle and creak beneath us, dovetailed, tight as a good wooden boat to carry us onward. And onward full tilt we go, pitched and wrecked and absurdly resolute, driven in spite of everything to make good on a new shore. To be hopeful, to embrace one possibility after another—that is surely the basic instinct... If

the whole world of the living has to turn on the single point of remaining alive, that pointed endurance is the poetry of hope.[3]

* * *

These words reflect the journey that Rekha and I made to move from grief to hope, healing, purpose, and love. Susan said that we will continue to live with chronic sorrow, the mixture of sadness and joy that we began to recognize in the second year of our grief. We had to learn to live with those two opposing emotions simultaneously, and each year it becomes more natural. I have also heard this process called post-traumatic growth. The trauma of Shreya's loss surely made us grow in that painful way. It was very tough and remains so today. We thank Shreya for giving us the opportunity to take that growth journey.

Chapter 2

A New Journey: Launching Our Foundation

There is nothing noble in being superior to
some other man. The true nobility is in being
superior to your previous self.
—Hindu proverb

My business management and chemical engineering
training taught me to look for simple, real-life examples
to help me understand and communicate complex
concepts. Post-traumatic growth falls into a class of
complexity that requires a kind of special help. In the
commercial manufacture of chemicals, an important
ingredient called a catalyst never becomes part of the
final product. But without it, the manufacturing would
proceed at a miniscule pace. After the product comes

out, the 'spent' catalyst regenerates and is recycled to keep the chemical reaction going. For Rekha and me, the chemical engineer was Susan, her therapy was the catalyst, and the chemical reaction and product she made was post-traumatic growth. But she needed a container in which that growth could be produced. She wanted the container to be strong and sturdy so things would not spill out or spoil, and she identified our faith to be that container. She made a very thorough and sincere effort to create that growth in that container and give it to us.

Side by side with Susan's therapy, our Hindu tradition helped guide us through our grief and point the way forward. We drew on a philosophy of life that inspired us to turn a very traumatic situation into a calming and positive one. This transformation later resulted in the launch of the Shreya R. Dixit Memorial Foundation.

Hindus believe that everything happens for a reason, that life and death are a continuum, and that whatever we do in this world is due to a pre-ordained plan. Rekha and I believe we were destined to be born into our specific families, to become husband and wife, and to have a child who would leave us young. There was a purpose behind the life experience that has unfolded for us and that only a sacrifice like Shreya's would have given us. After losing Shreya we joined hands with new friends, local and national leaders, and great individuals who work tirelessly on safety and driving issues, and none of that would have happened if Shreya had not been lost.

Shreya came into our life to show us this path and then leave. Even though she was the younger of our two daughters, she guided our destiny. Our tradition says that we are all reborn, that death is a part of life in a never-ending cycle. The word 'death' is a misnomer; death only comes to the body, while the consciousness within us remains. The consciousness that took the form of Shreya may have appeared young in terms of her physical age, but she was probably a very mature soul. She gave us a wider purpose for living that began with the foundation and is now expanding through this book and every other medium that will help bring new awareness about distracted driving, turn the high-tech tide toward safety, and save lives.

Our first action out in the community sprang from Rekha's idea for organizing an awareness walk. She knew that the Susan G. Komen Foundation, the breast-cancer charity, had started small with fund-raising walks that had eventually grown into the famous 'Race for the Cure' that takes place in cities across the country. "Why can't we organize a walk like the Komen Foundation?" Rekha asked me. She began planning the first walk, an event dedicated to raising awareness about distracted driving. We also received inspiration from another Hindu tradition, the Raksha Bandhan.

Raksha Bandhan is a centuries-old Indian festival celebrating the ties of love and protection that bind a brother with his sister. *Raksha* is a Sanskrit word meaning 'protection,' and *bandhan* is the verb meaning 'to bond.' In the Raksha Bandhan tradition, a sister ties a ceremonial thread on her brother's wrist and prays for his protection and safety. The brother reciprocates with a pledge to be there for his sister whenever she needs him. A simple cotton thread therefore binds brothers and sisters in an inseparable bond. Rekha's idea was to encourage a bond between drivers on the road. During the walk, participants would take a pledge promising to drive distraction-free in order to protect each other and the community. As a symbol of their pledge—and in the spirit of Raksha Bandhan—each person would receive a handcrafted Raksha 'protection' wrist band.

While making plans for the first Raksha Walk, we also began to talk about forming a foundation dedicated to raising awareness about distracted driving. We took the idea to our next session with Susan, and she suggested we contact a friend of hers, Lynette Lamb, a Minnesotan who was working with a program to support girls in Pune, India. Lynette came to our home and we discussed how we could create a foundation that made a difference. That brainstorming conversation lit a spark of hope and anticipation about what we could accomplish, and we knew we had found our new mission. On August 17, 2008, nine months after we lost Shreya, we held our first Raksha Walk and began creating programs that would one day be part of the foundation that would bear her name. Shreya was reborn as a movement to eliminate distracted driving behavior. We set out to nurture the foundation just like we would have nurtured Shreya.

Our first initiative after the walk targeted college-bound high school seniors in an attempt to creatively engage them with the issue of distracted driving. We offered two $1,500 scholarships to winners of an essay/song contest on the theme of distracted driving. We eventually realized that it would be more beneficial to involve all students, not just seniors, so after three years of these scholarships we redirected our efforts to students enrolled in driver's education classes. Rather than reward two students, we could offer several driver's ed scholarships that would pay for approximately half of the course tuition. This way we could reach students who would be staying in the community for a while rather than seniors who were already driving and getting ready to leave for college. The younger high school students would then have two or three more years to get involved with our work, the Raksha Walk, and spread the word about distracted driving among their peers and family. Since then, our driver's ed scholarships have been awarded for poetry, videos, songs, essays, and other creative works to spread the message of distraction-free driving.

As we geared up for the first Raksha Walk on the first Saturday of August, 2008, in Eden Prairie, Minnesota, I worked on convincing the state to declare that day 'Distraction-Free-Driving Day.' I felt like I was throwing a stone in the dark at first, but as I spoke to more people the idea gained traction. We submitted the application and continued to find supporters to help us make our case. Governor Tim Pawlenty signed the first proclamation, which became the forerunner to three more proclamations observing the day of the Raksha Walk over the next three years. This tradition continues today with Governor Mark Dayton. In 2015, the foundation earned its eighth proclamation.

Distraction-Free-Driving Day gives the media an opportunity to highlight the latest facts, data, and research about distracted driving—as well as the Raksha Walk. Minnesota Secretary of State Mark Ritchie gave us a major boost when he agreed to be the guest speaker at our third walk, and we have expanded our visibility and reach each year since.

Rekha used her vision of a creative way to bring people together on this issue and together with our supporters we made it a reality. The Raksha Walk is infused with the spirit of friendship, protection, and commitment to the common good. It is a time set aside for remembering all the lives that were lost and the tens of thousands who were injured in moments of distraction on the road. It puts a spotlight on our own driving habits and allows people of all ages and walks of life to make a promise to protect each other on the road through our own mindful driving. Everyone leaves with items that will remind them of their commitment throughout the year, including the Raksha wrist band and a pledge card that reads:

> I PROMISE… To remember that everyone on the road is someone's sister, brother, mother, father, daughter, son or friend; to keep my eyes and mind on the road at all times— TO PROTECT YOU.

After the third successful walk in Minnesota, we launched the annual Raksha Walk in Simsbury, Connecticut, where Shreya was born and where we lived before moving to Minnesota. Thanks to the support of our large network of friends and supporters in that state, our application to declare the day of the walk Distraction-Free-Driving Day in Connecticut was also accepted and proclamations have been signed by the governor every year. True to Rekha's belief that we can start small and grow like the Komen Foundation, the Connecticut walk proved that our strategy is sound and it works.

After achieving success on the East Coast and in the Midwest, we aspire to launch a Raksha Walk in the southern U.S. and the West Coast.

The first milestone of our work to develop the foundation came in 2009 when we got an invitation from U.S. Secretary of Transportation Ray LaHood to meet with him and participate in a press briefing at the first Distracted Driving Summit in Washington, D.C. That summit, sponsored by the U.S. Department of Transportation and chaired by Secretary LaHood, validated distracted driving as a national epidemic. As the keynote speaker at the summit, Senator Amy Klobuchar from Minnesota showed that our state was at the forefront of a movement to combat distracted driving. She also showed her support by acknowledging our fledgling foundation and Shreya's story in her address.

The following year the Shreya R. Dixit Memorial Foundation received its 501(c)(3) status, making it an official non-profit organization. As a formal entity we began to enlist broader financial support from companies and organizations including AT&T Corporation, AAA of Minneapolis, CIGNA, Wells Fargo, Lean Horizons Consulting, Guardian Wealth Advisors, and Myslajek Limited. We formed working partnerships with the Minnesota Safety Council (www.minnesotasafetycouncil.org), Minnesota Office of Traffic Safety (dps.mn.gov/divisions/ots),

Minnesotans for Safe Driving (mnsafedriving.com), the City of Eden Prairie (www.edenprairie.org), Eden Prairie Women of Today (epwt.org), and the local newspaper, the *Eden Prairie News* (edenprairienews. com). Our dedicated board inspired a flock of volunteers who make the Raksha Walk happen in Minnesota and Connecticut every year.

Our first major media exposure came in 2009 when Minneapolis Star-Tribune reporter Kate Freeman interviewed me for a front-page article in the Sunday paper.[4] Minneapolis/St. Paul television stations WCCO, KARE11, ABC, and KMSP began giving extensive coverage to our walks and other events. These partnerships helped create and publicize programs that we believe are making a difference.

In addition to the driver's ed scholarships, the foundation awards internships to high school students through its Youth Outreach Internship Program. These students are actively engaged in raising awareness about distracted driving and educating the community on this critical issue. Students receive a cash award for their services to the foundation, and the project supports the professional interests of the students while also educating young minds on the importance of advocating safe driving.

The foundation's new public service announcement (PSA) category in the EDU Film Festival, Minnesota's statewide high school film festival, is another youth-focused program. Launched in 2015, this project was formed in partnership with the EDU Film Festival and the Independent Film Project of Minnesota. High school and college students up to age 21 are invited to create sixty-second (or less) PSAs about distracted driving, with screenings for semifinalists and finalists and a grand prize of an approved college-level production or screenwriting course at the Institute of Production and Recording (IPRS) for high schoolers. The rules for the video entries emphasize the message of the foundation by prohibiting actions such as filming while driving, engaging anyone to perform unsafe activities in a moving car, or glamorizing violence. Eight student filmmakers received awards in the first contest in 2015. A link to the winning videos is listed in the Appendix.

The foundation broke new ground in online education by teaming up with Boston-based educational technology company Synaptic Learning to create the world's first Adaptive Massive Open Online Course (aMOOC™) for distracted driving. This learning tool adapts to the user's learning style, delivers tailor-made content to accelerate learning, and works on any tablet, smartphone, PC, or Mac. The modular design gives short, customized lessons that keep the user engaged, and the format allows anyone to learn on their own time with a choice of sixty-five languages. The foundation website invites experienced drivers, as well as beginners, to take this free course to conquer driver distraction. The link to this tool can also be found in the Appendix.

We also created a 'speakers bureau' of sorts, bringing together people who can talk about distracted driving at schools, conferences, and to other groups. These speakers (including myself) tell compelling stories, based on their personal experiences, about the real dangers of driving distracted.

All of these programs serve the mission of the Shreya R. Dixit Memorial Foundation, which is to champion the observance of safe and distraction-free driving practices, raise awareness in the community about dangers of distracted driving, and encourage drivers to be mindful of the safety of other drivers and passengers on the road.

The foundation works for us on two levels. It brings sanity and internal peace to me and my family, and in the process allows us to educate the community about an epidemic that is taking a lot of lives. And although a great deal of our focus is on teen and young drivers, our programs impact drivers of all ages—even those who are not yet old enough to drive. Kids who come to our walks get our message and remind their parents of what they learned that day. I have received phone calls from parents after a walk who say that when they picked up their phone to answer a call while driving, their son or daughter sitting in the back seat cried out, "No, Dad, don't you remember the pledge?" Young children also helped to spread our message one year when we showed our eight-minute video, "In a Split Second," to kids at a summer camp. After watching the film and talking about it with a few Eden Prairie Police officers, the six-to-nine-year-old kids were asked to draw something about what they had learned. Those images blew our minds, so we collected a few of them to create the 2010 Shreya R. Dixit Memorial Foundation wall calendar. It is never too early to start shaping hearts and minds about safety.

Carrying out our work with the Raksha Walk and our foundation is the best medicine to manage our grief. It gives us healing every day by bringing peace from the inside. The activities are external, but we have internalized them so that they serve as therapy for us. This works on multiple levels, such as the one in which I do public speaking. I speak from the heart about our personal tragedy, which never gets easier. But when I see people in the audience listening to me, I feel that something positive is happening. At the end of a talk or an event when someone comes to me and says, "well, you probably changed our thinking on this," or "we will definitely follow your suggestions," that means a lot. What started as a very uncomfortable effort slowly turned out to be highly effective therapy.

The annual walks that our foundation carries out in Minnesota and Connecticut are perfect examples of the combined joy and sorrow that Susan taught us to live with. We find joy in helping others share their stories of loss and find healing, but at the bottom of it, we are doing this because we lost our child.

Vijay Dixit & Antonia Felix

Chapter 3

Therapy is a Two-Way Street: Michael's Story

"No work or love will flourish out of guilt, fear,
or hollowness of heart, just as no valid plans
for the future can be made by those who
have no capacity for living now."
—Alan Watts

As time went on, the foundation's work started to get noticed in the community. We never dreamed we would affect lives the way we did, especially with a young man on the wrong side of the distracted driving epidemic. In the fall of 2014, a totally unexpected opportunity presented itself under the garb of a teenage boy. Why do I call it an opportunity? I'll explain later.

On an August evening in 2013, 20-year-old David Riggs was excitedly waiting for his girlfriend on his motor scooter near his driveway in the St. Paul suburb of Oakland, Minnesota. At the same time, and in a nearby neighborhood, 18-year-old Michael Vang was leaving to pick up his sister from work. When he got into his car, he placed his phone in the cup holder. Just a few blocks away from home, his phone lit up and he looked down to read the text. Three seconds later he looked up. "All I saw was a cracked window," Michael said. "I heard a huge thump. I was in shock—I didn't know what it was." He got out of his car to find a young man and his motor scooter lying on the street. And then Michael recognized him. "I had struck a friend," he said. David Riggs, a college student, had graduated from Michael's high school two years earlier, and Michael had always looked up to him. "Finding out it was someone I knew, and someone my sister knew, was devastating," Michael said.[5] He saw the shattered dreams of a young individual quickly unfold right before his eyes, and his three seconds of cell phone distraction were the cause.

A few hours after the crash, David succumbed to injuries in the hospital leaving his family and a large number of friends in extreme grief. In a split second, Peggy and Craig Riggs were forced to become members of the unenviable club that Rekha and I had joined eight years ago. As the father who lost his daughter to the irresponsible action of a distracted driver, I could just imagine the storm brewing at the Riggs' house.

Michael was charged and sentenced.

Just before the sentencing date, I received a phone call from a probation officer that surprised me. She told me that she was working on the sentencing phase of a distracted driving fatality case for a 19 year old. The officer reached out to me to find out if I would agree to have the young man perform community service for the Shreya R. Dixit Memorial Foundation under a court order. The victim family had requested this as an alternative to an otherwise more severe sentence.

That was a new and scary thought for me. I would be facing someone who would be a proxy for the young girl who caused the crash that killed Shreya. How would I handle it? I was torn.

But then an inner voice reminded me that I had always wanted to engage the young woman responsible for Shreya's death in our foundation's activities. I hoped that by involving herself with the foundation she would be able to heal from the trauma of the crash. Unfortunately, that never happened. So now, when the officer approached me, I felt I was getting a second chance to do exactly what I was unable to do eight years ago.

The driver who makes a fatal mistake by driving distracted must learn to live with that mistake. I suspect it was a big struggle for the driver in Shreya's crash, and it was not going to be any different for Michael. My inner voice commanded me to treat it as an *opportunity* as well as a challenge to do something in Shreya's memory.

I told the officer that I would work with Michael. I explained that I wanted to do more than simply fill up his required hours; I would take on the responsibility of transforming this young man from a distracted driver into a lifelong advocate for distraction-free driving.

I could have taken the easy path of having Michael do some administration and paper work for the foundation. Instead I chose to do something unique. My mission was to change his behavior for life, to help him grow as a result of his mistake and mentor him to influence other young drivers to adopt responsible and distraction-free driving habits. Metaphorically, I wanted him to pollinate good driving behavior seeds in the youth community.

I was aware that I had never received any counseling education or training. I had zero experience. How would I do it? But I reasoned that I had acquired a distinctive qualification in 'grief management' in the last eight years. There are so many in this world confronting numerous types of grief on a daily basis, but how many of them really consider that to be a qualification to counsel others? Perhaps I am one of those outliers who does. I believed it would be worthwhile to transform my so-called qualification into a form of self-therapy. I would not only be helping this teenager, but also healing myself in the process and blunting some of the sharp pain and grief that comes from losing a child. I called it customized grief therapy on steroids.

When I first met Michael he could barely communicate. He was terrified, confused, shaken, and lost. He silently observed as I brought him along to my speaking engagements and panels at high schools. Slowly, I began to talk to him about the crash and his feelings. Bringing him out of his shell, waking him up, was just the beginning. Over the next ten months, Michael transformed himself. He started to talk at individual teen panels about distracted driving.

Six months into my engagement with Michael, he agreed to schedule a teen panel on distracted driving at his alma mater. Another test for him came in August of 2015, at Shreya R. Dixit Memorial Foundation's 8th Annual Raksha Walk and Run. I asked him and he agreed to speak about his irresponsible action in front of an audience of more than 250 people of all ages. I also told him that Mona Dohman, the Minnesota Commissioner of Public

Safety, and Rob Reynolds, Chief of Police of the City of Eden Prairie, Minnesota, would be among those present at the event. I forewarned him that David's aunt and cousin would be there, listening to him. I am sure Michael expected to find himself in the middle of an environment that was similar to the heavy air that encircled him the day he crashed his car into David's motor scooter.

After all, he must have realized how painful and difficult his court-ordered community service was going to be. I assured him that I would not let him give up. I would be there to help if he tripped up.

To help encourage Michael about his speech, I told him the story of a friend's positive experience after giving his first talk about a painful topic. Former Minnesota Secretary of State Mark Ritchie and his wife Nancy are friends and supporters of our foundation. Their twenty-year-old daughter Rachel was killed by a drunk driver. Rachel had checked the box as an organ donor on her driver's license, and one year Mark was invited to speak about the importance of organ donation at a luncheon meeting. He told the story of his daughter's crash and the lives that were positively impacted by her decision to check that box.

After his speech a young man came up to him and told him that his dad had been on an organ waiting list and been passed up due to politics. The young man was angry as he told his story about how the program had mistreated his family, but then he told Mark that his speech had changed his mind. He pulled out his Michigan driver's license and asked Mark to be his witness as he checked the organ donor box on the spot. Sharing our stories, no matter how painful, can change lives.[6]

Michael gave a brief but honest message at the walk, and I was proud of him. With state officials and the members of the victim family in attendance, I know it was one of the most difficult things he had ever done.

I kept raising the bar on Michael. In fact, a few days after the walk, I gave him another tough assignment. I asked him to start drafting an apology letter to Peggy and Craig Riggs. He spent the next two months thinking about what to say, how to say it, and writing the letter. After Michael gave it to me I hand-delivered the envelope to Peggy and Craig at their house. They were not only surprised but very moved after reading the two hand-written pages. I am sure David's soul found some peace in Michael's gesture to his parents.

As we approached the conclusion of Michael's one hundred hours of engagement with the foundation, I sprung another difficult challenge on him.

Lindsey Seavert of KARE, the NBC affiliate in Minneapolis and Saint Paul, Minnesota, reached out and asked me to participate in a TV special she was putting together on the distracted driving issue. Lindsey expressed interest in using my mentoring work with Michael as the subject of her production. For that she wanted to interview both me and Michael. She also wanted to speak with Peggy and Craig Riggs.

Before saying yes to Lindsey I wanted to check with Michael to see if he was willing to own up to his mistake on TV. We talked about how a segment on the TV news would allow tens of thousands of people to hear his story and maybe be convinced to drive distraction free. After a bit of convincing, he agreed. We finished our last taping on October 6, 2015, one day before the end of my assignment with Michael. The show aired and received positive responses from the viewers.[7]

Michael's community-service assignment with our foundation ended on October 7, 2015. I was curious to know what the court system thought of my approach to working with him and if they felt I had accomplished what I had set out to do. Although I had submitted weekly progress reports on my activities to the post-sentencing probation officer, I really wanted to know her final assessment.

In my last conversation with the officer I asked if and how I met her expectations on the assignment. Her response was interesting. The reports showed that I was not engaging Michael in a typical way. She had expected me to delegate some foundation paper work and other routine non-profit volunteering activities to him to fill up the one hundred hours of community work. She did not expect me to mentor him, give him an active role as a public speaker, and help him heal. She did not envision that this nineteen-year-old would own up to an act that took a precious life and do something about it.

Working with Micheal turned out to be very therapeutic for me, which truly made our relationship a two-way street. I not only helped Michael comply with the law, but also received something of tremendous value in return.

I will tell more about Michael later, but for now, the first part of his story shows that the foundation intersects with people on all sides of the issue of distracted driving. Working with Michael transformed me and my vision for the foundation.

The foundation's mission is to help turn the tide of the distracted driving epidemic and heed one of the warnings that Shreya stenciled onto her bedroom wall when she was sixteen. Among the positive quotes and song lyrics that grace her walls are these lines from the rock band Incubus' song, "Warning":

When will we change?
Just in time to see it all fall down.
Those left behind will make millions writing
books on the way it should have been…

Our dear Shreya, we are not looking to get rich off a book or to look back at the deadly road on which our many distractions are taking us. Instead, we are setting up ways to help people change their behavior. *When will we change?* Thanks to the good work of our supporters and to all the distraction-free driving programs launched by businesses, government agencies, and groups throughout the country, we are changing *now*.

PART 2

Working Knowledge

Vijay Dixit & Antonia Felix

Chapter 4

The Distraction Epidemic

"Recent deadly crashes involving drivers
distracted by text messaging while behind
the wheel highlight a growing danger on
our roads."

—Excerpt from President Obama's 2009
Executive Order banning the federal work-
force from texting while driving

The crash that took Shreya's life happened in 2007.
How many others were lost that year?… that month?
How many keep dying every year? According to the
U.S. Department of Transportation, 10 percent of fatal
crashes in 2012 and 2013 were caused by distracted
driving.[8] In 2013, that meant 3,154 people were killed
in distracted-driving crashes. That is an average of

263 killed per month or 9 per day. Those are large numbers, but my family decided that even one death a day caused by a preventable crash is one too many.

The fact that you are reading this book shows that you are serious about driving safely in our high-tech world. You may not have time, however, to search online for the official data and statistics about distracted driving, so this chapter presents the basic numbers, which tell their own story. You can also find a list of online resources in the Appendix.

Nearly 80 percent of teenagers—the least experienced drivers on the road—own cell phones. One in four of them are 'cell-mostly' when it comes to going online, which means they use their phones instead of a laptop or PC to interact with Facebook, surf the Internet, text, or do any other web activity.[9] When those teenagers use their phones while driving, they are as impaired as drunk drivers (as are adults).[10] That's a fact. This combination of impairment, youthful inexperience, and distraction is a deadly mix.

Teenage and twenty-something drivers are the most likely to be distracted while driving, but adults of all ages are taking their eyes/attention off the road due to some kind of visual, manual, or cognitive distraction. One-fourth of teenagers answer one or more text messages *every time they drive*, and 20 percent of teens and 10 percent of adults carry on extended text conversations while driving.[11]

With 2 out of every 10 teenagers and 1 out of every 10 adults focused on lengthy text messages while they're behind the wheel, our roads are packed with drivers who are virtually blind. The average five seconds that drivers take their eyes off the road while they're texting equals, at 55 mph, driving the length of a football field blindfolded.[12] Those five seconds are an eternity for the thousands killed and hundreds of thousands injured in distraction-caused crashes every year. The largest population of drivers who are distracted when getting into a crash are under age 20—10 percent of drivers under age 20 who are involved in fatal crashes are distracted. Drivers in their 20s account for 27 percent of distraction-caused fatal crashes.[13]

Talking on a cell phone makes a driver
more impaired than driving drunk.[14]

One in four car crashes is caused by distracted driving. That number is shocking, but we never think it will happen to us. Throughout the country, real-life experiences bring another dimension to this 1-in-4 statistic, showing that a distracted-driving crash can happen to anyone. It can happen to even the most honest and ethical among us, like a man named Chris Weber who caused a fatal crash in Minnesota in 2014.

"1 in 4"—Chris' Story:
The Wrong Choice

Chris, an electrician, ten-year-member of the Army National Guard, and veteran of the war in Afghanistan, was driving down a rural county highway when he decided to use the time to call his bank. After one glance at his phone he heard a thump and pulled over. He had struck a woman riding her bicycle and pulling her two preschool-age daughters in a bike trailer. The 33-year-old woman, Andrea Boeve, died when the side of Chris' truck threw her into the ditch. Chris and a man who stopped at the scene tried to save Andrea, but could not. One of the girls was severely injured with broken ribs and a punctured lung, but both girls survived.

Chris pleaded guilty to vehicular manslaughter. From the day of the crash, he has admitted that it was his choice, a bad choice, that caused Andrea's death and shattered her family. Like so many of us, he ignored the risks and got distracted, never believing he would hurt anyone. "I never thought once it could be me," he said. "It never crossed my mind. All it took was one time. It was my choice that day. I was raised to be an honest person, so if you make a mistake, you own up to it. If you're honest, the punishment is not going to be worse than if you lied."[15]

Chris is serving a 12-month jail sentence that is broken up into three-month periods that will end in

2017. He was also sentenced to three hundred hours of community service and uses that time to talk to students and companies about distracted driving. He also helps the Minnesota State Patrol raise awareness about distracted driving and tells his story in a State Patrol video about distracted driving.[16] Chris says that talking about the crash is tough, but that it is usually easier to talk to high school students than the adults in the companies that invite him to speak. "The students listen better… they seem to care more," he said. "The young, driving-age students are more impressionable, and they listen."[17] A few students always come up to him afterward to thank him, often in tears. They tell him that they understand and appreciate that he is telling his story for their benefit.

Chris has had the most difficult time talking to people he knows, especially people at work. They have been supportive and understanding, but he was frightened about sharing his story with them the first time. "It was always my fear that wherever I go I would be judged," he said. "It was awkward to tell the guys I work with every day, and to this day it is still hard to talk to them about it."

Chris speaks to students and groups as often as he can to try to convince them to always make the good choice of focusing on driving. "Right from the get go I knew it was my fault and that I'm the one that could have made a different choice that day," he said. "Unfortunately, I didn't. I made the wrong one. My goal is to try to get people to understand and make the right choice."

Texting while driving raises your crash risk 23 times, according to an 18-month study of truck drivers.[18]

Looking, Doing, Thinking: The Many Types of Distraction

Cell phones and in-dash technology are not the only types of distractions causing this epidemic. Three categories of distraction sum up all the ways we can become impaired while driving: visual, manual, and cognitive (mental). A visual distraction takes your eyes off the road, and this includes looking at your phone to read a text, email, map, or see who is calling; watching your GPS or a video; or looking into your rearview or visor mirror or at your fellow passengers. Visual distractions may also involve non-avoidable situations like poor weather or bright sun. Manual or mechanical distractions include interacting with a cell phone by hand texting, dialing, using a navigation system, and adjusting a radio or any other type of electronic device. As our family learned, a manual distraction also includes reaching for a napkin. Of course, activities like holding a pet, eating, drinking, putting on makeup, and any type of grooming cause manual distraction by loosening a driver's hold on the steering wheel. The third category, cognitive (mental) distraction, is a complicated mix of visual, manual, and thought processes that hijack the driver's attention. Having a conversation with co-passengers or with someone on the phone, even when you're talking hands-free, takes your mind off the road in front of your eyes and creates cognitive distraction.

It is true that individually each of the above distractions can cause a fatal crash, but texting seems to be the most dangerous distraction of all. It involves all three types of distractions: visual, manual, and cognitive.

Here is where we get to the epidemic proportions: during daylight hours on any given day, about 660,000 American drivers are using a cell phone or other electronic device. Every time you reach for the phone, tap a button or punch in a number, or write out a text or email, you are *three times* more likely to get into a crash.[19]

A Disappointing Trend

Minnesota's Year-to-Date Fatal Crash Count

March 2015	March 2016
31	51

Source: Tim Harlow, "Stickers Latest Effort to Eliminate Traffic Deaths," *Minneapolis Star Tribune*, March 6, 2016

The Multi-tasking Myth

One of the most surprising facts about talking on a cell phone while driving is that there is no significant difference in the level of distraction between holding the phone and using a hands-free device or system like the car's Bluetooth connection. Even when hands-free, the mental process of engaging in a conversation is dangerously distracting. Just as surprising is the fact that talking and listening demand different levels of work in the brain. Talking—producing information—requires more brain power than simply listening, and that's where we get into trouble.

One of the nation's leading researchers on driver distraction, David Strayer, a professor of psychology at the University of Utah, explained that the brain does not focus on two things at once, but instead switches back and forth between tasks. This switching happens so quickly that we may think we're multi-tasking, but actually we are task switching. The brain is shifting its attention from one task to another. When the brain is focused on one task, like forming thoughts and language during a conversation, it may not be giving attention to the critical task of monitoring/scanning the road. Strayer designed a brain workload scale that ranges from 1 to 5, and the data from his research suggests that when we try to generate information, to talk, it takes the highest level of workload, category five. Trying to talk on a smartphone or a car audio system, or even to a passenger, forces the brain to throttle back and forth between talking and listening.[20]

If something unexpected happens while you're talking, you're not going to be able to respond to it quickly enough. The brain is so preoccupied with processing your talking that it cannot process what is in your visual field, causing 'inattention blindness.' A red traffic light or bicyclist may be right in front of you, but you literally do not see it because your brain is focused on the workload of talking. "The attentional network that is responsible for processing what you see around you is doing something else," Dr. Strayer said. "If you take your eyes off the road to do anything—to read, to dial, to surf the Internet, check stocks, or read newspapers, it causes problems and they start to crop up immediately. The data suggests that eyes off the road for more than 2.5 seconds increases the crash risk."[21]

Don Fisher of the University of Massachusetts-Amherst and David Strayer developed a model called SPIDER that defines what happens when someone talks on a cell phone while driving. The letters of the word stand for Scan, Predicting, Inattention blindness, poor Decisions, and Execute a Response:

> **Scan:** Scanning is a process of acquiring information to understand where you and others are. When you start to talk on a phone you tend to stare straight ahead more and

more, almost like a robot, instead of scanning. You don't look side to side or at pedestrians.

Predicting: A skilled driver begins to anticipate where hazards might be. If there's a school bus up ahead I'm going to drive a bit slower, and I scan for pedestrians at crosswalks. Good drivers are aware. Their accumulated skills keep them alert. But when you talk on a cell phone while driving, you stop predicting where hazards might be—you act like a novice driver. You throw away your expertise and ignore possible hazards.

Inattention Blindness: You don't see what you're looking at if you're not paying attention. When you are talking on a cell phone, your brain is focusing its attention on that task instead of processing what you see in front of you.

Poor Decisions: Safe driving is a conscious process. Talking on the phone compromises all the ways a driver makes good decisions.

Execute a Response: Talking on the phone while driving makes reaction times sluggish, delaying them by up to 30 percent, and this increases the risk of crashing. Higher speeds at the point of a crash make the crash more severe.[22]

The mental distractions described in SPIDER reveal how impaired a driver becomes while talking on a cell phone. As Dr. Strayer put it, "You become like Mr. Magoo, driving around without any clue of where you are on the road or what is around you. Then, if you react to something that requires your attention, you're not going to be able to do it as well."[23] Research done by Dr. Strayer and others tells us that even the slightest distraction, which reduces our 'situation awareness,' or knowing what is happening around us, can lead to poor performance behind the wheel.[24]

In addition to the impacts of talking while driving listed in the SPIDER model above, the physical act of looking at the phone causes many crashes. According to Minnesota Trooper Lt. Tiffani Schweigart, almost every crash she and her fellow officers see is a rear-end crash. And more and more frequently those crashes are due to cell phones. "There are not many injuries, fortunately, because the speeds aren't as high," she said. "But how do you hit somebody when the traffic is approaching a slow down on a long straightaway? You hit somebody because you're not paying attention. That's the only reason."[25]

Over the past decade, Dr. Strayer's world-renowned work has revealed shocking facts about the dangers of distraction. His studies have shown that hands-free and handheld cell phone conversations are equally distracting, that 'inattention blindness' sets in while talking, that talking on a cell phone makes teenagers and young adults react as slowly as elderly drivers, and that talking on a cell phone behind the wheel is like driving drunk.

The science that reveals the equal dangers of distracted and drunk driving is moving us toward a new mindset about our phones and other devices in our cars. Drunk driving is taboo in our society, thanks to public awareness and tough penalties and enforcement. One day, if we are successful in fostering change, driving distracted will also be taboo. We will look back at these days of talking and texting on our phones while driving as a time of blind and ignorant recklessness. But now that the facts are being heard, the distraction-free-driving movement is well underway.

A Survivor Who Beat the Odds

1 in 10 drivers ages 15 to 19 involved in fatal crashes in 2013 were distracted.[26]

In 2013:
3,154 people were killed in distraction-affected crashes
424,000 were injured in distraction-affected crashes[27]

The facts about distracted driving are shocking, but the numbers never tell the whole story. Distraction kills and changes the lives of survivors forever.

One young survivor whom I have had the good fortune to meet is a well-known distraction-free-driving advocate whose tragic story began on the day she graduated from college. On May 18, 2008, Jacy Good and her parents were driving home from her graduation ceremony at Muhlenberg College in Allentown, Pennsylvania. As they drove through an intersection at a green light, an 18-year-old boy talking on his cell phone ran a red light, which caused a semi-truck to swerve out of his way. The truck hit the Good's station wagon head-on and both of Jacy's parents were killed instantly. Jacy was alive but not breathing, and an off-duty paramedic who lived near the crash rushed over and re-positioned her head to clear her airway.

Jacy spent nine hours in surgery, but her injuries were so severe that her doctors didn't expect her to make it. In addition to broken bones and internal injuries throughout her body, she suffered from a traumatic brain injury that gave her a mere 10 percent chance of survival. But she surprised them all.

It took years for Jacy to learn to walk, speak, and feed herself, and to this day she is still learning how to manage some of the basics of life. Her left arm does not function, and her left leg does not fully work. She is filled with rods and metal, wears an ankle brace, and still has memory problems. But she is vibrant, happily married to her longtime boyfriend, and a deeply committed advocate for distraction-free driving. She speaks at conferences, visits companies and schools, and appears in videos and in the media.

With years of talks behind her, Jacy finds, like Chris Weber, that teenagers seem to take the message most seriously. She has observed that the kids are ready to drive distraction free, but their parents are not:

> Overall, teenagers seem to get this. The question they ask most often is how they can stop their parents from driving distracted. I hear so many stories of kids begging their parents to stop, but they won't stop. I encourage them to tell their parents that they made a new friend, Jacy Good, and she lost both of her parents. Then they can ask, 'What would happen to me if we got in a crash right now?'[28]

Those parents may have a sense of false safety with all the in-dash technology and entertainment systems in their vehicles. As more of that distracting technology becomes 'normal,' we tend to believe that it must be safe. We assume that car makers put a priority on safety, but when it comes to distraction, they are ignoring the way the human brain works. Jacy believes that this blind spot is out of step with the history of car makers' focus on safety:

Car companies have always worked toward making cars safe. Back when the first cars were built they didn't want to install windshield wipers because they thought it would be too much of a distraction. The original distracted driving was looking at your wipers—car makers thought you would be hypnotized by them. Today car manufacturers keep improving air bags and creating systems that can detect someone coming into your lane, but for some reason they won't focus on distraction. It just doesn't make sense.[29]

In 2012 and 2013:
10% of fatal crashes were caused by distraction
18% of crash injuries were caused by distraction
16% of all crashes were caused by distraction[30]

---

480 bicyclists and pedestrians were killed in accidents caused by distracted drivers in 2013.[31]

In a 2014 survey of American drivers, more than one-third (36.1%) said that they read a text or email while driving in the past month, and more than one-fourth (27.1%) said that they typed a text or email.[32]

The Numbers Up Close:
One State's Distraction Figures

In January 2016, the Minnesota Office of Traffic Safety released the latest state figures about distracted driving. Conducted in the summer of 2015, the Minnesota Distracted Driving Survey aimed to assess the prevalence of distracted driving behaviors and create baseline data for future studies.

Distractor	Percent Distracted	
	MALE	FEMALE
Cell Call	4.7	4.0
Cell Handling	5.3	3.9
Reaching	1.1	2.4
Smoking	2.0	2.2
Passenger Front	0.5	2.2
Passenger Back	14.3	8.4
Drinking	1.4	1.9
Eating	1.1	3.6
Other	0.6	0.8

Figure 1. Types of Distraction Observed on MN Roads in the MN Distracted Driving Survey (2016) (dps.mn.gov)

A group of researchers moved around to a total of 201 predetermined sites to observe drivers of cars, vans/minivans, sport utility vehicles, pickup trucks, and small commercial vehicles. Thirty-one of the sites checked stopped traffic, and the remaining sites checked moving traffic.

The researchers observed 11,471 drivers during the survey period. An amazing 29.14 percent of the drivers were distracted.[33] The highest distraction rates occurred on Mondays and Saturdays (Figure 2), and throughout the week the peak hour for distraction was between 5:00 and 6:00 p.m. (Figure 3).

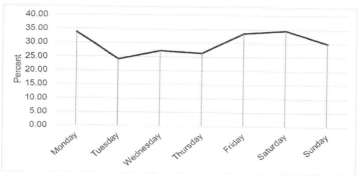

Figure 2. Distracted Driving Across Days of the Week—Minnesota Distracted Driving Survey (2016) (dps.mn.gov)

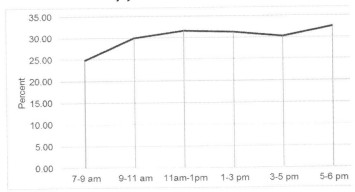

Figure 3. Distracted Driving Across Hours of the Day—
Minnesota Distracted Driving Survey (2016) (dps.mn.gov)

Are men or women more likely to drive distracted? Does age affect the numbers? And what kinds of vehicles are found to be driven by the most distracted drivers? According to the survey:

- Male drivers (30.2 percent) were more likely to be distracted than female drivers (27.6 percent)

- Teen and young adult drivers (ages 16–29) were the most likely to be distracted (35.5 percent)

- Drivers of vans/minivans were the most likely to be distracted (37.6 percent) followed by drivers of pickup trucks (31.4 percent), SUVs (28.5 percent) and passenger cars (26.3 percent)

The observers saw drivers handling cell phones in 4.8 percent of all vehicles, which, extended to the number of drivers on Minnesota roads in any given hour, means over 18,000 drivers are handling their phones while driving. They observed 4.4 percent of all drivers making calls on their phones, which means almost 17,000 drivers on Minnesota roads at any given hour are talking on their phones behind the wheel.

As distraction research around the world tells us, conversations create inattention blindness in drivers, whether those conversations are on the phone or with passengers.[34] Based on that, the survey also looked at the numbers of passengers and conversations:

- Approximately 30 percent of vehicles included occupants other than the driver

- Active conversation was recorded 48.5 percent of the time

- Rear seat passengers were in conversation with the driver in 11.9 percent of all vehicles (this would involve over 45,000 vehicles on Minnesota roads in any given hour)

- Front seat passengers were in conversation with the driver in 1.2 percent of all vehicles

As speed and congestion increase, so
does the prevalence of distraction.
–Minnesota Distracted Driving
Survey (2016)

The observers found that the rate of distraction varied between city and country areas. While fewer distracted driving behaviors were found on rural roads, the percentage of distracted behavior in both areas is alarming:

- The distracted driving rate for the seven-county Minneapolis/St. Paul metro is 30.9 percent

- The distracted driving rate for rural Minnesota is 27.5 percent

- Drivers on local roads (20.3 percent) were less likely to be distracted than those driving on secondary (31.2 percent) or primary (35.1 percent) roadways

This recent Minnesota survey confirms that our roads are unsafe at any speed. With nearly one-third of us driving distracted, we make it routine to risk our own lives and those of other drivers and pedestrians every day. We take the complex process of driving for granted and accept distraction, especially with devices and conversations, as the new normal. We must learn from the numbers, the science, and the tragedy of distraction-caused crashes and reject this behavior. Empowered with the facts, we can choose to respect ourselves and everyone else on the road and drive distraction free.

* * *

The first step in solving a problem is acknowledging that it exists. The daily fatal crashes and alarming statistics are solid proof that distracted driving is a lethal epidemic. The next step is weighing the options for the best solution.

Is technology the answer? Will phone companies, auto manufacturers, and tech entrepreneurs create a fix? The second option is the legal approach. Will tough laws on the local, state, and federal level change people's habits and turn the epidemic around? Or what about the third option, education/raising awareness—are training programs the answer to changing mindsets and behavior? Or will the answer be a combination of all three?

Vijay Dixit & Antonia Felix

Chapter 5

Combating Distraction with Technology

"Our inventions are wont to be pretty toys, which distract our attention from serious things."
—Henry David Thoreau, *Walden*

"We see it all."

When it comes to distracted drivers in Minnesota, nothing would surprise Col. Matt Langer, Chief of the State Patrol. "We recently drove past someone with an iPad on the steering wheel, playing a game," he said. "There's all kinds of craziness we see behind the wheel." To Matt and everyone at the Minnesota Department of Public Safety, most car infotainment systems, cell phones, tablets, and other devices are not improving our quality of life as we get from here to there, but damaging it. Anything that distracts from driving is a threat to the life of fellow travelers.

Not everyone considers in-car technology a risk, however. A *Consumer Reports* video claims that infotainment systems are "safer, less distracting than picking up your phone." [35] That statement is misleading at best. As Dr. Strayer's research shows, the difference in distraction between using a handheld and hands-free phone while driving is tiny—talking hands free is only 0.18 less distracting on his mental workload scale (see Figure 4.).

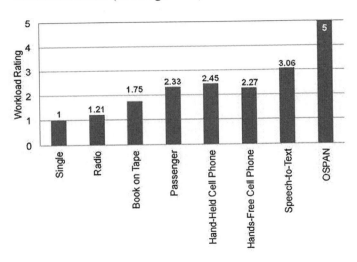

Figure 4. The mental workload required for a variety of interactions with technology while driving, based on David Strayer's research. (OSPAN at the high end of the scale reflects a mentally demanding numbers-and-word task, to anchor the high end of the scale.)[36]

The *Consumer Reports* comment not only gives a false impression of hands-free safety, but also clashes with Col. Langer's outlook, a perspective based on years of observing crashes and deaths caused by distraction. It also seems to represent the auto industry's attitude about the 'safety' of voice command and other hands-free systems.

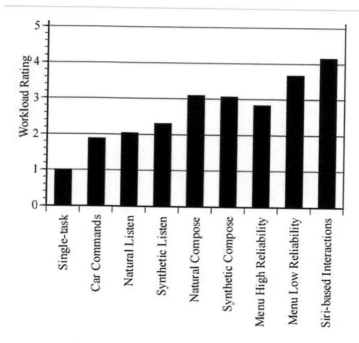

Figure 5. Workload ratings for interacting with voice-activated, hands-free technology while driving.[37]

Talking on the phone while driving increases the 'workload' of the brain and shifts attention away from the task of driving. David Strayer developed a rating system that shows the mental workload levels of nine distraction-causing activities drivers may experience. In Figure 5, we see that speaking and listening to iPhone's Siri, a hands-free voice system, ranks near the top of the workload.

The risk of hands-free, voice-activated technology in the car comes with what the mind is asked to do, such as create questions and thoughts. When the brain is doing this work, it cannot pay adequate attention to anything else. Inattention blindness is a fact of life, and I find it difficult to believe that designers, engineers, and executives in the auto and technology industry are not acutely aware of the risks associated with it.

It perplexes me to think that, knowing these risks, they continue to integrate more distraction-inducing technology into new cars.

Car manufacturers now integrate high-tech, crash-avoidance systems that warn you when you get too close to the center line, the car ahead, any objects behind you, and anyone in your blind spots. They also must follow federal standards for safety features such as seatbelts, air bags, windshield defoggers, head restraints, brake system standards, and mirrors, *but there are no regulations that address cognitive distraction.* When it comes to avoiding the inattention blindness caused by in-dash technology, why are automakers only given 'voluntary guidelines?' Something seems to be falling through the cracks in regulatory oversight.

The U.S. Department of Transportation (DOT) and the National Highway Traffic Safety Administration presented those guidelines in 2013 to assist automakers in designing car controls.[38] These guidelines included:

- Limiting the time drivers must take their eyes off the road to perform any task to two seconds at a time and twelve seconds total

- Disabling the following operations unless the vehicle is stopped and in park:
  - Display of text messages, web pages, and social media content
  - Manual text entry
  - Video-based entertainment and communication such as video phoning

The guidelines explain that these recommendations are based on research that "strongly suggests that visual-manual tasks can degrade a driver's focus and increase the risk of getting into a crash up to three times."[39]

Are automakers listening to these suggestions or considering the research that has been available for the past few years? Let's take a look at some of the 'connected car' systems available in today's new cars.

Built-in Car Infotainment Systems

Most newer cars include some type of connectivity, from the simplest—an auxiliary jack that can connect your phone to the stereo system—to a full-blown, touch-screen system like Tesla's that eliminates all the knobs and dials in the car. In between are phone-connected systems that handle GPS, music, and many applications.

Each generation of in-dash systems seems to be getting more user-friendly, with larger buttons and simpler menus, but some are still prone to crashes, require too many menus to sift through, and do not respond well to touch.[40] One journalist who covers the automobile industry wrote that when it comes to infotainment, "it's still pretty much the Wild West. There are some really good systems, and there are some really bad systems out there."[41]

Since texting is the riskier distraction on the road, I am always surprised to learn about the text options in infotainment systems. The Chevrolet MyLink system, for example, includes a 'Text' icon among the large icons on the main screen.[42] When your phone is connected to the system, a new text alert will come up on the screen. You can only choose the 'View' option if the car is not in motion, but while driving you can choose 'Listen' or 'Dismiss.' You can also select an automatic reply from a list. Chevrolet says that the 'Listen' response is the most popular, and the large, clear button to press for that selection seems to take the two-second rule into account. But it is important to point out that according to Figure 5, listening to a 'synthetic' voice such as a system-read text (or GPS directions) is slightly more distracting than listening to a natural voice. Many of us often find ourselves talking back to the synthetic voice when the GPS fails to decipher our own voice command. That is a very distracting activity.

The text system in Ford's MyFord Touch system also gives three options for responding to a text alert, but unlike the Chevrolet system, the driver can respond by typing a text if the car is going three miles per hour or less.[43] I believe that this sends a message to drivers that it is OK to text as long as you are going very slowly or stopped in traffic or at a light. Every state except Texas, Missouri, Montana, and Arizona bans texting while driving, so this 'loophole' in infotainment systems is out of step with state laws. In Minnesota, for example, it is illegal for drivers to text or interact with the phone's touch screen even when stopped at a traffic light.

The text system in Cadillac's Cue technology actually allows the driver to read a text rather than just listen to the system read it. The text appears on the main infotainment screen and a small screen behind the steering wheel where the driver is usually glancing at speed, gas, and temperature readings.[44] By giving the driver access to the text message, the Cue system ignores the federal guideline about disabling the display of messages, web pages, and social media content when the car is in motion.

The most admired infotainment system in the industry may also be the most distracting. The Tesla touchscreen is a seventeen-inch-long panel that controls all the car's systems, replacing every knob and button on the dashboard. This system is in a class by itself, and not just in terms of its size. Drivers have full access to an Internet browser while driving, which means moving the eyes to the right to read website pages that fill up the screen. Drivers definitely use the feature. An advertising company examined Tesla car data in 2013 for a month to see what drivers were reading on the web. They discovered that more than half of their web-reading choices were news sites, followed by financial news, sports, and various entertainment sites.[45]

The Tesla screen is the size of two iPads and can be viewed in a split-screen mode to view two systems or applications at the same time. Tesla may be breaking new ground with its Auto Pilot feature, which allows the car to stay in its lane while on cruise control, but in terms of distraction, the company seems to be shifted in reverse. What were Tesla executives thinking when they envisioned drivers looking over at the huge console to read the *New York Times* while driving their otherwise masterfully engineered electric cars down the freeway?

Doctor Strayer's most recent research sponsored by the AAA Foundation for Traffic Safety put the latest infotainment systems to the test. He studied the mental workload of interacting with systems in ten different 2015 car models, with drivers using only voice-commands. The results showed that each of the interactions required a moderate to high level mental workload (averaging 3.34 on the 5-point workload scale). The rating system took into consideration the intuitive, complex, and time-consuming qualities of each voice-command task. Figure 6 shows how each car measured up. The least distracting system was Chevrolet's MyLink system in the Equinox, and the worst-rated interactions were with Mazda's Connect system.

Vehicle	Workload Rating
Single Task	1.00
Chevy Equinox	2.37
Buick Lacrosse	2.43
Toyota 4Runner	2.86
Ford Taurus	3.09
Chevy Malibu	3.39
VW Passat	3.46
Nissan Altima	3.71
Chrysler 200c	3.77
Hyundai Sonata	3.77
Mazda 6	4.57
OSPAN	5.00

Figure 6. Mental workload ratings of using voice commands to interact with 10 different 2015 model cars.[46]

Older drivers experienced a significantly greater workload when using these systems. The study also found that practice with the car over a week did not make the difficult operations any easier. Researchers were surprised to find long-lasting 'residual costs' after the interactions—it took 27 seconds for drivers to return to the baseline 'single-task' state after interacting with a voice-command task. Over that length of time, a distracted driver travelling at 25 MPH would cover more than the length of three football fields.

This important experiment shows us that "just because a driver terminates a call or text message does not mean that they are no longer impaired," Strayer wrote.[47] To prove this point, just think about how you feel after quarreling on the phone with a friend, spouse, parent, or someone from work. A moving vehicle is not a substitute for the kitchen table, restaurant booth, or office cubicle where such conversations normally take place.

Like automakers, cell phone carriers and third-party developers make it easy to connect devices hands-free, and provide applications that they claim are cutting down on distraction.

Phone Applications

At first glance, an app that blocks texts and calls and starts automatically when the car moves, sounds like the perfect fix to cell phone-induced distracted driving. That is the idea, according to Sprint, AT&T, and Verizon, but a closer look reveals that these apps are all teeth and no bite.

Like all three carriers, Sprint offers its application, Drive First, for free. The app kicks in when the car reaches the speed of ten miles per hour, and parents with teen drivers can set it to not be disabled or deleted from the phone by securely making that setting with a PIN. Once activated, the app blocks texts and can be set to send an automatic reply.

So far, so good. But another feature allows three of the phone's apps to function while in Drive First mode. When I explored the set up options on my phone, I realized that I could choose texting, Facebook Messenger, and Twitter apps, all of which ignite the highest level of distraction. Even with the savvy parental control function, this feature renders the app useless.

Verizon's Safely Go app includes the same faulty feature, allowing the user to choose any three apps to run while the app is engaged in blocking texts and calls. In addition, rather than turning on automatically, the app must be manually switched on every time the driver wants to use it. This asks a lot of a teenage driver or anyone whose phone has become like another limb.

The strongest of the three, AT&T's Drive Mode, only allows navigation and music apps to run, and launches when the car reaches 25 miles per hour. Like the other applications, the driver can program a small number of phone contacts whose calls will not be blocked.

More text- and call-blocking applications are available on cell phone app stores for little or no charge. And if you use a stand-alone GPS or do not need road guidance, there is always the option of turning on 'airplane mode' to turn off calling, texting, and data. Like the Verizon app, however, this means being proactive about making the effort when you get in the car.

Phone carrier applications are not exclusively designed for teen drivers. Drivers of all ages can benefit from a driving-phone-free app that is used with real commitment. But since teenagers are the heaviest users of cell phones and other devices while driving, these applications can play an important role in curbing their use. Before taking a look at a few more types of (so-called) distraction-reducing technology, let us stay with the teen driver issue. Brain science is beginning to understand why teenagers, more than people of any other age group, get caught up in risky behavior that can lead to crashes.

Technology and the Teenage Brain

While technology in the car increases everyone's risk of having a crash, this risk is even greater for teenagers. Road accidents are the #1 cause of death among adolescents throughout the world. In the U.S., teens are about three times more likely than people over twenty to have a fatal crash, and six teens die in crashes every day.

The simple explanation is that teens are the least experienced drivers. But new research into how the teenage brain works shows us that teenagers are also much more likely to take risks behind the wheel than adults. When texting, calling, playing with social media, bringing friends along for the ride, and other distractions are added to this risk-taking behavior, the danger skyrockets.

Teenagers undergo dramatic changes in brain development, second only to the changes that happen in early childhood. Sarah-Jayne Blakemore, a leading neuroscientist specializing in adolescent development, explains that these changes include a greater drive to take risks.[48]

Teens are headed toward adulthood and need to explore the world to find their own place and sense of security. And exploring means taking risks. Adolescents are driven to become independent of their parents and turn toward their peers for approval and a sense of belonging. This is why, according to research by Blakemore and others, the social brain of a teenager is ultra-sensitive about social feedback.[49]

Two aspects of teenage brain development create this risk-taking attitude. First, the brain's chemical reward system, including the feel-good chemical dopamine, is at its peak. Adolescents are hyper-sensitive to cues about a potential reward and fired up with anticipation about getting those rewards. When teenagers get positive feedback from their friends and others their age, their brains light up with 'happiness' chemicals.[50]

At the same time, the teenage brain is a long way from mastering impulse control and other decision-making abilities. These higher thinking functions that take place in the prefrontal cortex are not fully mature until at least the mid-twenties. Researchers point out that the imbalance between these two areas—a highly active rewards system and immature impulse-control system—may explain why teenagers take more risks than children or adults.[51]

These insights shed new light on the statistics about teenage car crashes. Now that we know why teenagers are so sensitive to what their peers think about them, we can understand why they ride together, talk in the car, and try to impress each other with risky behavior.

One experiment about the impact of passengers on teen driving used a simple stoplight driving game in a driving simulator. Researchers measured the brain activity of the participants as they made decisions about what to do at an upcoming intersection with a yellow light. Three groups of drivers—adolescents, young adults, and adults, played the game, and during some rounds the players knew that their friends were watching them on a monitor in the next room.

The results showed that the teenagers took significantly more risks when their friends were watching. They made more go-through-the-light decisions and had more crashes than the young adults or adults, who also knew that their friends were watching. The peer 'presence' also caused the teenage brain 'reward prediction' centers to light up, while the older drivers' brains did not behave that way. When driving 'alone,' all three groups behaved about the same (see Figure 7).

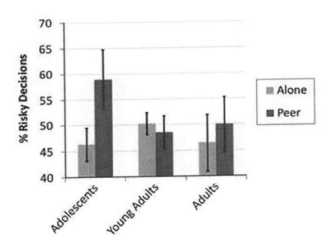

Figure 7. A stoplight game experiment showed that adolescents made dramatically more risky decisions when they knew that their peers were watching them.[52]

Studies like these reveal why more crashes occur when teenagers drive with their friends in the car. We now know that:

The presence of teen passengers increases the crash risk of unsupervised teen drivers. This risk increases with the number of teen passengers.[53,54]

When teens drive with teenage passengers, they use risky driving practices like speeding, not wearing seatbelts, keeping shorter distances to the vehicle ahead, and being inattentive (looking but not 'seeing' the road ahead).[55]

The mere presence of a passenger, even without talking, makes teenagers less attentive drivers.[56]

Some studies have found that the negative impacts on driving are stronger when both the driver and passenger are males.[57]

The massive level of reward-center activity in the teenage brain brings up another challenge. David Strayer is concerned that social media, texting, and other activities are addictive to teenagers. "My biggest concern is that some of this tech is likely to be addicting," he said, "because it's tapping into rewards circuits."[58] Teenagers may be wired to feel as if they *have* to respond to texts and calls and constantly check their Facebook timelines. Strayer hopes that we will soon see studies about this possible connection between teenage behavior with devices and the unique development of the teenage brain.

Hardware Solutions

The most serious approach to disabling cell phone distraction, other than tossing the phone in the trunk, involves installing a piece of hardware that automatically connects to software on the phone and launches when the car moves. These products, such as Cellcontrol, are web-based, which means they can be customized on a home computer or laptop to allow and disable your choice of applications. By choosing password-secured settings online, parents can ensure that their teenage drivers cannot interact with texts, calls, games, or social media, but still use their phones for GPS and to make and receive calls from selected contacts.

These products also allow parents to receive information about how their teenagers are driving. The system acts like a monitor, delivering reports about speeding, braking, accelerating events, and other actions. Research shows that these phone-blocking systems work best when parents are able to receive feedback about their sons' and daughters' driving that they can then discuss with them.[59] Nichole Morris, the principal researcher at the University of Minnesota's HumanFirst Laboratory, who studies teenage driving and distraction, explained how monitoring through these systems can alert parents to a teen's distracted driving. "If the notification says that your teen went through a stop sign at forty miles per hour, that probably means he or she was distracted."[60] But if the system shuts down the phone to everything but making 911 calls, how could the teen be using the phone? More on that in a moment.

The University of Minnesota's HumanFirst Laboratory ran a study about the effectiveness of phone-blocking software on teen drivers who had just received their drivers' licenses.[61] A hardware sensor mounted in the car automatically launched the software on the phone when the car began moving. Once the teen began driving, the software blocked all calling (except 911), texting, and other applications. In one of the three experimental groups, the software also reported driving behavior alerts to parents. After taking the state's required class about Minnesota driving laws, all three hundred teen drivers in the study knew that talking on a cell phone is illegal for drivers under age 18 and that texting while driving is illegal for all ages.

The groups with the blocking software on their phones called and texted much less than did the control group, whose phones only recorded their use rather than blocked it. But how did the novice teen drivers with the blocked phones manage to call or text at all? About 15 percent of them figured out how to bypass the system by either starting a phone call before getting in the car or downloading apps that ran in the background on the phone. In addition, some of the drivers borrowed a phone from a friend who was in the car.[62]

This study proved that a well-designed, phone-blocking system can dramatically reduce calling, texting, and other phone use among teen drivers. Even though some drivers found a way to bypass the system, Figure 8 shows how well the blocking software reduced texting compared to the teen drivers whose phones were not blocked (top line). The fact that the drivers felt compelled to break the law, and in some cases outsmart the system, is another example of how the adolescent brain is prone to impulsive and risk-taking behavior.

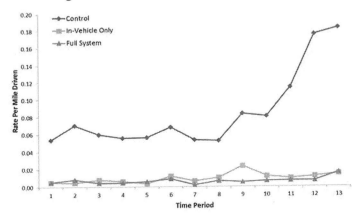

Figure 8. The average texting rates per mile of novice teen drivers, from the Minnesota Teen Driver Study. Even though some of the teenagers found ways to bypass the system, the phone-blocking software designed by the

study had a strong effect in eliminating or
curbing texting. The top line represents teen
drivers who did not have blocked phones.
All the drivers had taken the state's required
class about Minnesota driving laws and knew
that texting is illegal for all drivers.[63]

Nichole Morris is convinced that the best use
of technology to solve cell phone distraction is
automated technology.[64] Her lab is developing a
commercial version of the automatic phone shut-
down and monitoring system used in the teen study
in hopes that it will be available as an effective
option for ending phone distraction in teens. But as
an expert on distraction research, she is convinced
that technology alone is not the most dangerous
threat to the novice driver. Since teens are prone to
risky behavior, and having peers in the car increases
teen crash risk exponentially, she believes the rules
about passengers should be more strict.

The hundreds of new teenage drivers Dr. Morris
recruited for her study took driving seriously, wanted
to be safe drivers, and were more than happy to
participate in something that was going to make
them safer. She believed that these first-time drivers
did not intend to be risky, but when passengers are
present teenage drivers start engaging in more risky
behavior. "If I could just push an easy button I would
restrict passengers more," she said. "In Minnesota
you can drive with one non-sibling passenger for six

months. We assume that after six months these new drivers are so much more responsible and jump to allowing three passengers. We know that's just not true." The research is clear about teen passengers and crash risk, she explained:

> For a male teen driver, with each added male passenger it's not even a linear relationship to fatal crashes; it's an exponential crash risk with the addition of each male passenger. The reason for that is you have this group think—'Isn't it fun if we all speed,' or 'Let's not wear our seatbelts, none of us!' There is very reliable research on this. For females it obviously goes up as well, but the effect is not as large.

> Males are more likely to speed, and speed is a major risk factor. You layer a little distraction on that and teens will easily lose control of the vehicle. And they may not all be buckled.

> We don't want driving to be the last fun thing a kid does.[65]

Hardware gadgets, firmly installed in the car, may be the only fix for drivers who cannot resist answering calls, texts, emails, and social media alerts. A device that can shut down a phone as soon as the driver starts the car, relieves the driver of making decisions about how to interact with the phone. For most drivers, this type of solution may completely eliminate one form of distraction among the many that come up in every drive.

Head-up Displays

A transparent GPS map floating on the lower part of your windshield is bound to be less distracting than one on your phone or console, right? That is the logic behind head-up displays (HUDs). Many of these products are for navigation only, projecting arrows for upcoming turns, lane recommendations, the speed limit, current speed, and time to destination. The driver can hear the spoken directions through the cell phone speaker or wireless connection to the phone.

Some HUDs, however, also project texts, notifications, music app controls, phone contact IDs, and other information for drivers to read and respond to. The makers of the Navdy HUD tell us that "any notification on your phone (text, social, etc.) can be displayed, read aloud or disabled entirely. Decide what you want to appear when."[66] After paying $499.00, drivers may be enticed to use the full range of the device. Besides, the driver in the official Navdy video assures us that it makes the car as safe as an airline cockpit: "It's a heads-up display just like what commercial airline pilots use when they're landing," he says. "You hear that? Pilots use it. It's safe."[67]

Deborah Hersman, who served three terms as chairman of the National Transportation Safety

Board (NTSB), disagrees with that appraisal. The NTSB investigates airline accidents and other major transportation events, making Hersman one of the nation's top experts in aviation safety. She knows that pilots are not more focused than drivers and that aviation-like controls do not guarantee safety. "We have investigated events where pilots were texting while they were taxiing and, distracted by their laptops, would overfly their destination by one hundred miles. A pilot who was flying an emergency medical services helicopter was texting. While flying he crashed and killed everyone."[68] Pilots are not infallible; they're human. And technology is only as 'safe' as the user's behavior.

Device makers claim that HUDs lessen distraction because drivers never take their eyes off the road while looking at the transparent display. As we know, however, mental distraction is not about where your eyes are looking, but about what your mind is doing. That is why psychologists who study distraction, like Paul Atchley at the University of Kansas, call HUDs "a horrible idea." In spite of all the research about the dangers of cognitive distraction, HUD technology, Atchley said, "is driven by a false assumption that seeing requires nothing more than having the eyes fixed on the right spot."[69]

Vocally composing a text to respond to one that just popped up on the HUD increases the driver's mental workload to over three on the scale in Figure 5. Even though hand gestures allow the driver to answer or reject a call without pressing anything, the cognitive distraction of interacting with text on an HUD still creates inattention blindness. In fact, HUDs may be even more dangerous than other devices, since the straight-on position may give drivers the confidence to look at the words, numbers, and images for longer periods of time.

Much like HUDs, wearable devices, or head-mounted displays (HMDs), narrow the distance that the driver's eyes must move. Google Glass, an HMD that looks like a pair of glasses without lenses, places a small, square pane of information just above and in front of the wearer's right eye, and uses voice-activated technology. Costing over $1,000, this gadget was also marketed as a safe alternative to using smartphones while driving. A 2014 study led by Ben D. Sawyer at the University of Central Florida compared the distraction caused by using a smartphone to Google Glass. Even though Google is no longer actively marketing this product, similar devices are being developed and sold, so this research is timely and important.

The Google Glass driving-simulator study revealed that both devices are almost equally distracting. Whether using a smartphone or wearing the Google Glass headset, the participants drove with poor lane keeping, slower reactions, and less headway. "Most importantly," the researchers concluded, "for every measure we recorded, messaging with either device negatively impacted driving performance."[70]

Sawyer and his fellow researchers commented that HUDs have a lot of potential if they can be used, for example, to sense when drivers are getting tired. But in terms of distraction, 'multitasking' with a smartphone or Google Glass creates a mental overload that takes the mind off driving. "Forward vision does not necessarily guarantee forward attention," they wrote. "In other words, watching the roadway does not mean a distracted driver will react to events that occur on it."

Is Technology the Answer?

Drivers have always listened to the radio, talked to passengers, reached for things, eaten, sipped coffee, or put on makeup while behind the wheel, but cell phones and built-in technology increase the odds that the driver will *always* be interacting with something. Auto engineers and phone carriers do not yet consider distraction-free cell phone use a serious safety issue, so it is up to each individual to make the right choice.

The bright displays that are now standard in new cars make distraction activity the new norm. Auto manufacturers follow the law, but not the facts about how our minds handle tasks like reading, speaking, and listening. The inattention blindness that impairs us when we interact with in-dash technology causes crashes, but carmakers insist that they are safer because they are hands-free. Besides, they are in the business of giving customers what they want. General Motors' Chief Infotainment Officer Phil Abram justifies onboard tech as simply a way of life. "Smartphones are a part of people's lives," he said. "If we claim to be a customer-centric organization, if we truly are, then we gotta say, hey, that's important in their lives. We have to make sure that it works, and we work with it as best we can."[71]

While the science tells us that even the latest hands-free, voice-command interactions are highly distracting, organizations like the American Automobile Association (AAA) Foundation for Traffic Safety are optimistic about their ability to help automakers make positive changes. Jake Nelson, Director of Traffic Safety Advocacy and Research at the AAA Foundation, is confident about AAA's approach. About three weeks before the foundation releases a new piece of research, Jake and others give a briefing to automakers and those who make the in-dash infotainment hardware. These briefings give the industries a heads-up about the latest research, giving them time to think about how they may or may not consider applying it and how they will respond once the news hits the media. Some executives have gone to Jake and his team privately after those briefings and asked if they can meet with their engineers and provide information about how to design safer products. Some, on the other hand, don't even want to admit that they could make their products safer.[72]

The AAA Foundation prefers to work with industry rather than trying to get the federal government to enact new regulations. "The people who know how to do this right are not in government," Nelson said. "They are engineers. We can work most effectively if we work with the people who know how to make it work." Nelson asks the regulators to work with the AAA foundation and with the industries to do the right thing.[73]

I see a somewhat disappointing trend in the current technology space. Safety advocates question executives and decision makers at conferences and trade fairs about the rationale for risk-prone features offered by car companies, consumer electronic producers, wireless service providers, non-OEM (original equipment manufacturers) device makers, and cell phone app developers. Their standard response is that customers want such products and businesses must meet those expectations. That may be true, but corporations are also expected to self-monitor their offerings to ensure the safety and well-being of the customers they serve. However, under the guise of customer satisfaction, both large and small corporations seem to compromise corporate responsibility. This is not the first time our country has faced such dilemmas over ethics, morality (producing products harmful to our health with no warnings), and profits. Contentious debates in the tobacco and alcohol industries took place in the 1970s and led to strong regulations about advertising and marketing those products.

We do not need to go through the same experience again. As Jake Nelson of AAA explained, safety organizations can build a collaborative environment between industry and consumers with a goal to develop products that make money for manufacturers *and* keep consumers safe. The AAA Foundation has shown leadership in that area by proactively reaching out to industry players about potential safety issues and product deficiencies before publicly releasing its information. The foundation has had success with this approach, giving manufacturers a chance to address deficiencies beforehand and save themselves from bad publicity and potential loss of business.

Work like this convinces me that when it comes to creating the technology that drivers use every day, corporate responsibility and profitability can co-exist.

Vijay Dixit & Antonia Felix

Chapter 6

Outlawing Distractions: Just the Ticket or Not Enough?

"The key to tackling distracted driving comes down to three things: good laws, good enforcement and getting people to take personal responsibility."
–Ray LaHood, U.S. Secretary of Transportation, 2009-2013[74]

The Good Fight

The story of car safety laws in the United States begins in 1956 with a second-year Harvard Law School student interested in researching automotive safety. After Ralph Nader started practicing law, he continued his research and developed an outline and a few chapter sketches for a book. In 1965 he found a publisher, and *Unsafe at Any Speed: The Designed-In Dangers of the American Automobile,* became an instant bestseller. Nader's book exposed the 'immoral' behavior of automakers in neglecting to put doable safety measures into their designs. The book led to public outrage, congressional hearings, and just ten months later, the launch of a new federal agency, the National Highway Safety Bureau, now the National Highway Traffic Safety Administration. A new era of safety regulations had begun, and in 1968, carmakers were required to include seatbelts in every new car.[75]

Providing new cars with seatbelts did not mean that people would start wearing them, however. States did not begin passing seatbelt laws for nearly two decades—New York was the first in 1985. Most other states (except New Hampshire, which still only requires children under age 17 to wear seatbelts) passed their own laws throughout the rest of the 1980s and 1990s. These laws, as well as visual and beeping seatbelt reminders, the national "Click It or Ticket" awareness campaign, toughening the laws, and other factors, steadily drove up seatbelt use. In 1994, the seat belt use rate was 58 percent, and by 2014 it had climbed to 87 percent.[76]

The seat belt laws in 34 states and D.C. are *primary* laws, allowing officers to stop a driver and issue a citation when they see an unbelted person in the car. Fifteen states have *secondary* seat belt laws, in which officers can write tickets for non-seatbelt use only after the officer has ticketed the driver for another offense, such as expired registration tabs or speeding. When states changed their seat belt laws from secondary to primary, seatbelt use increased. Twenty-eight states and D.C. have also passed laws, either primary or secondary, that require passengers to wear seat belts in the back seat.[77]

As safety regulations increased, from air bags to shoulder belts and child safety seats, crash fatalities across the nation went down. Today, wearing a shoulder-and-lap seat belt and driving a car equipped with air bags reduces crash fatalities by almost 50 percent.[78] Thanks to lawmakers who listened to public demands, these safety features have become a way of life for many drivers, and since 1975 more than 255,000 lives have been saved by seatbelts alone.[79]

Laws have also reduced the number of drunk driving deaths on the road. Like the story of the first regulations given to automakers, the tale of tougher driving-under-the-influence (DUI) laws starts with one person. In 1980, Candy Lightner of Fair Oaks, California founded Mothers Against Drunk Drivers, or MADD, after her 13-year-old daughter was killed by a drunk driver while walking down her quiet suburban street. The 47-year-old driver had been on a drinking binge after being released on bail for a hit-and-run arrest two days earlier. On top of that, he already had three DUI convictions on his record.

When Lightner learned that the drunk driver would probably get a light sentence, if any at all, her grief turned to anger. "This was not an 'unfortunate accident,'" she said later. "Cari was the victim of a violent crime. If my daughter had been raped or murdered, no one would say of the killer, 'There but for the grace of God go I.' Death caused by drunk drivers is the only socially acceptable form of homicide."[80] Lightner, a divorced mother with two other children, vowed to make her daughter's needless homicide count for something. She quit her real estate job and founded MADD with a twofold mission: to raise awareness about the seriousness of drunk driving and to fight for tough laws against it.[81]

With her growing volunteer network, Lightner pushed for a national minimum drinking age (states set their own limits of 18 or 21), and age 21 became the law of the land in 1984 with the National Minimum Drinking Age Act. Another milestone came with the group's successful push to reduce the blood alcohol level that defines intoxication from .10 to .08. The organization worked for decades to change society's attitude about drunk driving and claims that, since 1980, its efforts have saved 330,000 lives.[82]

The legal approach to distraction caused by cell

phones and other devices is making ground, but just as in the case of seatbelts and drunk driving, effective laws come gradually and take years of work. The latest milestone came with federal legislation passed in 2015. Thanks to lawmakers like U.S. Senator Amy Klobuchar from Minnesota and her bipartisan partners, anti-distraction resources were included in the 2015 transportation bill signed by President Barack Obama.

As the senator described in her Foreword to this book, every state now has access to funding for educating drivers about the crash risks and other facts about distracted driving. The new legislation is a major step, but it is only part of the solution. "No single law or set of laws is a silver bullet to end distracted driving," Klobuchar said, "but distracted driving laws can help curb this epidemic. My legislation incentivizes states to act to address distracted driving head on."[83]

Senator Klobuchar's commitment to distraction-free driving is motivated by her concerns as a parent and the tragic realities of distraction-caused crashes in her home state:

> As a mother of a college student, driver safety is something that is on my mind literally every day. Over the years, I've heard so many stories of families who have lost loved ones because of distracted drivers. Just this past April, a twenty-five-year-old driver was

reading a text message when she hit and killed a forty-year-old mother of two who was out for a bike ride with her sister in Glencoe, Minnesota. Heartbreaking stories like these remind us that stopping distracted driving is a matter of life and death.[84]

While laws about distracted driving help the public understand the seriousness of the issue and, at times, convince people to stop using their phones and devices behind the wheel, the legal approach has its challenges. State law enforcement agencies do not have enough resources to fully enforce the anti-distraction laws that are finally on the books. Let's take a look at those laws.

Distraction is a Crime

Currently, 46 states, D.C., Puerto Rico, Guam, and the U.S. Virgin Islands ban text messaging for all drivers. All but 5 have primary enforcement of the texting ban (an officer can stop a driver for this violation alone). Of the 4 states without an all-driver texting ban (Arizona, Montana, Missouri, and Texas), Texas and Missouri prohibit text messaging by novice drivers and Texas restricts school bus drivers from texting.

Talking on a cell phone with the phone in hand is illegal in 14 states, D.C., Puerto Rico, Guam and the U.S. Virgin Islands. Using a speaker or other hands-free system with the phone is not against the law except, in many states, for young, novice drivers, who are prohibited from any kind of cell phone use. Figure 9 shows where handheld phone use is banned.

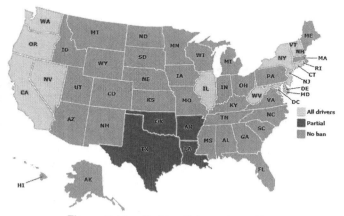

Figure 9. Handheld cellphone bans.[85]

A Death Worth 90 Days

Fines and sentences vary from state to state and county by county, but we can get a general idea of the legal process in a fatal or serious injury distracted-driving case by using Minnesota as an example.

If a driver in Hennepin County, Minnesota, is ticketed for texting while driving, he or she will be charged with a petty misdemeanor $50 fine the first time. After the first offense, the fine is increased by $225, regardless of the number of offenses. Texting while driving could also be the basis of a misdemeanor charge of careless driving where the maximum sentence is 90 days in jail and up to a $1,000 fine.[86] If a driver is texting and kills someone, there is a possibility of a charge of criminal vehicular homicide. Where the distracted driver causes great bodily harm in a crash, there is the possibility of a felony charge of criminal vehicular operation. If the injury is less serious (bodily injury), there is the possibility of a gross misdemeanor charge of criminal vehicular operation. Assuming alcohol is not involved in each of these instances, the state must prove that the driver was operating the motor vehicle in a grossly negligent manner.[87]

Proof of gross negligence due to distraction can be hard to prove. In many cases, a prosecutor will not have the evidence necessary to establish the gross negligence required to charge the driver with a felony or gross misdemeanor. Instead, the offender faces the maximum sentence for regular misdemeanor careless driving: 90 days in county jail, assuming carelessness can be established.[88]

Anti-distraction advocates in Minnesota are pushing for a longer gross misdemeanor sentence of up to a year in jail if someone dies as a result of careless driving, but as of this writing in 2016, the maximum is still 90 days.

A prosecutor may be able to establish a case for a felony if, for example, a passenger testifies that the driver was texting or surfing the Internet when he or she caused the fatal crash. But in many cases, according to Robert Speeter, an attorney who practices criminal defense in Minnesota, no one witnessed the distraction, and most drivers are probably going to minimize the distraction aspect of the crash.

"This is the practical reality of the law at the moment," Speeter said. "We can't test for distraction like we can for alcohol. There is always a possibility that a phone could record the timing of a text to prove that the driver was texting at the time of the crash, but even if the driver consents to a search, the phone is most likely to be encrypted and the prosecutor is probably not going to get at the information. The prosecution can subpoena phone records from the phone carrier, but at best it will show a record of texts sent and received, but not establish the exact moment of the crash. If Apple's iMessage or another Internet-based messaging service is used, there is likely no record of the message that can be retrieved from the carrier."[89]

In one recent case in which the state *did* get access to a driver's phone records, the texting driver was charged with a felony. On an October afternoon in 2013, 24-year-old Stephanie Deloye was driving her SUV in Minnetonka, Minnesota, when she struck a 57-year-old woman who was crossing the road at a marked crosswalk. Witnesses said that the SUV never slowed down before it hit the woman. When the police approached Deloye's car, they saw her cell phone in her lap, and it was turned on. She initially denied that she was texting when she struck the woman and told police that her windshield pillar obstructed her vision. After the police analyzed her phone records, which showed that she had received and responded to texts at the time of the accident, she admitted that she was texting. The woman Deloye hit was seriously injured with multiple fractures of her pelvis.[890] Deloye was charged with a misdemeanor for careless driving and sentenced to twenty-five hours of community service and restitution of any outstanding amount of the victim's $12,000 hospital bill that was not covered by insurance.[91]

The Deloye case is more the exception, Speeter explained, because texting is often difficult to prove and harsher sentences usually come where death or injury is caused by a person with either intent to hurt the person or with well-recognized reckless conduct such as drinking and driving as opposed to 'mere' carelessness.[92]

This sentiment of the law—and of society— is important, because everyone understands that accidents happen. It explains why offenders like Chris Weber, who admitted from the start that he was distracted by his phone when he struck and killed the bicyclist on a country road, receive a one-year jail sentence for a felony. Those county jail sentences can be carried out in many ways, such as the typical work-release in which the offender goes to work all day and spends the night in jail, or electronic home monitoring.

Since so many drivers use their phones behind the wheel, a crash like Weber's could have happened to anyone. It was a tragic, heartbreaking crash, but accidents happen. Only by altering society's perception of distraction as a free-will choice with a high risk of harm and even death, will the laws begin to change. If making the choice to text or read websites while driving becomes as taboo as making the choice to drink and drive, laws will change. Even more important, people will be less likely to make the wrong choice.

Minnesota Trooper Lt. Tiffani Schweigart believes a wave of public support for tougher laws is growing stronger. "I get calls from the public a couple times a week saying, 'I'm sick of seeing distracted drivers—are you doing enough to stop them?' So they are recognizing the severity of the problem, and there is a lot of community support," she said.[93]

Lt. Schweigart also believes that tougher anti-distraction laws will change behavior just as drunk-driving laws do. When drivers know that officers are watching and ready to enforce the law, they often make better choices. For example, when Lt. Schweigart and her fellow troopers patrolled an area known for potential DWI (Drinking while Intoxicated) offenses one evening, they saw first-hand how their presence changed drivers' behavior. After 2:00 a.m. that night, they noticed that a bar's parking lot was filled with cars, even though the bar was closed. The patrons did not drive themselves home because they knew the officers were focusing their patrol on that area that night. Schweigart believes that when the public has the same feeling about driving distracted, they will choose not to use their phones in the car. "The public has to believe they're going to get caught," she said.[94]

Officers like Schweigart who witness crash scenes every day know that without a change in the culture's mindset, drivers will continue to use their phones behind the wheel. That change may come with tougher laws, higher awareness about the risks of distraction, a wide use of phone-blocking technology, or a combination of all three. But until then, the crashes are becoming more common. In a recent case that Schweigart discussed with the press, a 17-year-old teenager was posting to Facebook when she ran through a red light. She struck a car and killed the driver and his 10-year-old daughter. According to the report, the passengers had complained to the driver many times to stop using her phone and yelled out, "Red light! Red light!" before reaching the intersection. "What a senseless behavior that caused all of this trauma to this family," Schweigart said, "using a phone while operating a motor vehicle, 3,000 pounds of mass, through an intersection, tearing this family apart."[95]

It takes time for the legal system and laws to catch up with society's demands for safety. How much longer would it have taken automakers to install safety belts if Ralph Nader had not exposed the industry's deliberate safety negligence in his book? How many more tens of thousands of people would be killed by drunk drivers each year if MADD had not spent decades fighting for laws? Now it is our turn to fight for greater public awareness about distracted driving and tougher laws to drive home the seriousness of the harm caused by distracted driving.

Watching the Phone, Crossing the Line

State patrol troopers who work to keep our roads safe battle against distracted driving every day. The new normal of phone use, coupled with the inadequate number of officers on the road, make enforcement a tough challenge. "In an amazingly short period of time," said Minnesota's State Patrol Chief, Col. Matt Langer, "the issue of texting while driving has become like drinking coffee while you're driving—it's what you do. It seems like almost everybody's doing it. Yet we're only an agency of nearly six hundred troopers, while there are about 3.5 million licensed drivers in the state of Minnesota. It's daunting and it's frustrating." The troopers don't have tools to help them attack the problem like they do with radar for speeding and the breath test for drinking. And they find that a lot of people aren't truthful. When a trooper on patrol sees a driver looking at a phone and stops him or her for it, often the driver won't admit to texting, but will say instead, "No, I was looking for a phone number."[96]

Since texting is difficult to detect, troopers are reverting back to issuing citations for the careless and dangerous driving conduct they observe. Langer explained that if a car goes over the centerline, the trooper may stop the driver and say, "I saw you were looking down... you were looking at your phone." "No," the driver may say, "I wasn't." The trooper then writes up the citation for going over the centerline. Langer believes they are doing a good job with this approach, not arguing whether the driver was texting or not, but focusing on the dangerous driving behavior. "We will probably be more successful going that route," he said, "than trying to ruthlessly witness what they are doing with their cell phone. We have proof of driving over the centerline. We have a hard time proving texting."[97]

We know that under the right conditions, such as having a large number of troopers focusing on certain roads for an extended time period, we can curb texting and keep the roads much safer. When the state's resources are concentrated in this way, such as in the 2014 I-90/94 challenge over four days every August, the effects are enormously positive. Thanks to drivers taking the 2014 Challenge seriously, a long stretch of Interstate across Minnesota was safer over those four days, and there were no fatal crashes. Drivers in Minnesota and along thousands of other miles of I-90/94 across 14 states coast-to-coast wore their seatbelts, drove more slowly, drove sober, and paid attention. "We can have an amazing impact with dedicating resources to a certain stretch of roadway," Langer said. "Consolidating our resources for maximum impact can make a profound impact for shorter bursts, but we can't sustain it three-hundred-sixty-five days per year."[98]

Like drinking coffee, texting is a way of life that drivers do not want to put aside when they get into the car. Langer thinks we may have crossed the line with this new lifestyle, and that we have technology to thank for that. "The iPhone changed what we do in our lives," he said. "I think iPhones and smartphones contribute to anxiety—it's addictive, an absolute psychological response. Our whole world revolves around it; we do so many things on that phone, but texting while driving is incredibly dangerous."[99]

Pushing for Safety at the State Capitol

Ramping up laws about texting, Internet surfing, video game playing, and other tech-induced distracted driving may sound like common sense, but the road there will be long and arduous. Perhaps no one in Minnesota knows this better than Nancy Johnson, the driving force behind Minnesota's graduated driver license law, which went into effect in 1999, and other important driving legislation.

Nancy Johnson is a founding member and former president of Minnesotans for Safe Driving, a non-profit organization that helps crash victims navigate the legal system, educates the public about drunk and distracted driving, and lobbies for safe-driving laws. Nancy and her husband became passionate advocates for safe driving after their 18-year-old daughter, Tina, was killed by a drunk driver who hit her head-on at 90 miles per hour on a country road.

In the 1990s, Nancy lobbied the Minnesota legislature for a graduated driver license law that would impose more restrictions on novice drivers. The first six months of teen driving are the most dangerous, and this law, like others around the nation, was designed to give drivers more privileges as they gained more experience. The proposed system that became law is divided into three stages that provide a learner's permit (driver must always be accompanied by a licensed driver), provisional licensure (allows unsupervised driving but with limits on passengers and nighttime driving, and no phone use), and full licensure.

Giving extra guidance to new drivers for at least the first six months is the least a state can do, according to the graduated driver approach. As the Minnesota program points out, we educate our children in reading, writing, math, history, and science for twelve years, but only give them six hours behind the wheel.[100] But the legislators needed a lot of convincing. "It was a hard sell," she said, involving six or seven years of work to finally see it pass.[101] Issues like curbing when and with whom a teenager can drive get personal, even at the most professional level.

"The *Star-Tribune* supported it and lots of people supported it," Nancy said. "But you get into the legislature, and you get a legislator who has a teenager and does not like the idea of that kid needing to get a ride with a friend and can't. It's an inconvenience." Across the state, legislators were outraged at the idea of limiting a few aspects of teenage driving for six months. "Rural legislators were adamant about it," she said, "complaining that their teenagers would not be able to double date or go to football games together. It was so personal. Nobody seemed to care about the safety of their kids—it was all about what was most convenient."[102]

Many who work with traffic safety have come up against this attitude. Gordy Pehrson, the traffic safety coordinator with Minnesota's Office of Traffic Safety, calls convenience the 'C' word. In the office's Point of Impact Program, where parents learn about teen driving risks and laws, Gordy and his team try to focus on one statement. "If they leave that program with any message permanently imbedded in their brain, it's that they need to make decisions about their teen drivers that place safety as a priority over convenience. But so many times parents just want to get their teens licensed so they don't have to take them to hockey practice." He often brings the point home by talking about the real-life consequences of distracted driving. "I use Vijay as an example almost every time," he said. "I tell them that I work with too many people who have had to bury their children, which is more inconvenient than saying no to your teen or having to take them to hockey practice."[103]

In spite of the uproar over the inconvenience of basic limits on novice teen driving for the first six months, Nancy Johnson persevered with her call to action, making her case one legislator at a time. On New Year's Day, 1999, a three-phased graduated driver license program became state law.

Laws like this one, as well as lowering the intoxication level for 'aggravated' DWI penalties, happen because people like Nancy dedicate their lives to taking action. It is not the easy path, or the painless one. "Every day I live with the fear of another phone call, a knock on the door and being told, 'there's been an accident,'" she said. "Oh God, I couldn't make it through that again. My friends think I am back to normal now because I laugh and joke and do familiar things again. However most don't know the emptiness, the pain and the loss I feel. Every day there are reminders of what happened and then the thoughts of what life would be if Tina were with us today."[104]

Nancy Johnson's long experience in lobbying for stronger safety laws gives her a broad perspective on the general attitude toward these laws. "Our government is not particularly interested in traffic safety, in my opinion," she said. "That's why it's such a battle. Here in America we have a lot of people who don't like being told what to do."[105] She is not alone in that perspective. In a focus group about distraction that we held with safety officials and experts, Frank Douma, the director of the Hubert H. Humphrey School of Public Affairs at the University of Minnesota, talked about the American driver's attitude. He compared it to that of people in some European countries, where complying with traffic laws is a stronger part of the culture. In the United States, he said, "some people feel that once they're in the car, they are the ones in control of their safety, regardless of what the law or other people are telling them to do."[106]

That attitude is working against us, especially in the case of texting behind the wheel. Officials know that much more texting and driving goes on than the numbers show, simply because drivers are not always forthcoming about texting if they get stopped or cause a crash. Each year in Minnesota, one in four crashes involves distracted or inattentive driving, resulting in at least 70 deaths and 350 serious injuries.[107] But according to Gordy Pehrson, the statistics about distraction-affected crashes are underreported. "If an officer responds to a crash, let's say it's a rear-end crash and the officer asks the driver what caused the distraction, that driver is less willing to volunteer information that might implicate him or her."[108] "Unless it's a serious injury or a fatal crash," he explained, "an investigation isn't going to take place in that respect. Patrol officers have not yet found a reliable way to report the real numbers, which is one of today's most difficult challenges in traffic safety."

In terms of the 'independent' American attitude, Paul Aasen, president of the Minnesota Safety Council, believes that a personal sense of responsibility plays a role in how we think about traffic laws. "Whether it's something you *should* do, or whether it's something that's required under the law, or whether it's something that makes you safer, the issue is about thinking, *It's just something I should do to become a cooperating and integrated part of this society,* Aasen said. "Every country in the world has laws, but without a rule of law with a compliance structure and ramifications, or a cultural desire to comply, you don't get a strong attitude toward obeying laws."[109]

Leading-edge Ideas About Distraction and the Law

In the future, laws about texting and other distracted behavior will become more nuanced as we see more and more distraction-related cases. For example, holding a remote texter liable for a crash has just begun showing up in the courts. Art Kosieradzki, a trial lawyer who represents crash victims and speaks to high school students about distracted driving, described the remote-texter liability idea. "If I absolutely know that you're driving and I initiate a texting conversation," he said, "and we're engaged in it, and the driver gets into a crash, do I have a responsibility for that crash? I think I do. I think the courts need to hold the remote texter liable because he or she is a participant." Art sees no difference between the remote texter and someone sitting in the back seat who physically reaches forward and covers the driver's eyes for four to five seconds every ten seconds or so. Four to five seconds is the average time spent on a text.

In 2013, the remote texter issue was actually brought to an appeals court in New Jersey. The court ruled that a remote texter could have a legal 'duty,' or responsibility, to avoid texting someone who is driving. Although the ruling did not apply to the remote texter in that case, it opened the door for such cases to be made in the future. If it could be shown that the sender had a 'special reason' to know that the receiver of the text was actively driving and reading the texts, the sender could be liable.[110]

"When the sender knows that the text will reach the driver while operating a vehicle, the sender has a relationship with the public who use the roadways similar to that of a passenger physically present in the vehicle," the court wrote. The court felt that remote texters are a threat to public roadways: "The texter has a duty to users of the public roads to refrain from sending the driver a text at that time."[111]

Even though he cannot often prove it, distraction is involved in many of Art Kosieradzki's cases. "We see this constantly," he said. "Sometimes we can view the traffic video of the driver with his head down, obviously looking at his phone. But even without that kind of proof, just going on the description of certain types of crashes, it is fairly evident what happened. It's senseless, and in my practice it doesn't seem to be getting better; it's getting worse."[112]

As people learn more about distraction, inattention blindness, the number of crashes caused by distraction, the mental workload of having conversations behind the wheel, the dangers of taking just two seconds to reach for something, and stories about crashes caused by people who use a phone while driving just like they do, attitudes will change. Drivers will become more aware of the risks and demand more safety from automakers and device manufacturers. When public opinion changes, laws and even systems change. The emotional trauma in the aftermath of a crash puts another layer of stress and anxiety on the legal process that both sides must undergo, and some are convinced that even that can change. Attorney Bob Speeter, for example, is dedicated to bringing a more humane approach to the court system by asking prosecutors to allow the two parties in a crash case to talk to each other early in the process. He has seen the positive impact that such meetings can have on everyone concerned, such as in the case of a fatal crash that took place about ten years ago:

> My client was driving an all-terrain vehicle, intoxicated, and taking the back roads where he thought he was safe. He carried three passengers in the two-person ATV. When he suddenly went in reverse and then hit the brakes, one of the passengers fell out the back and crushed his skull. My secretary

knew the victim family and knew that they were not resentful. I asked the prosecutor to do something very unusual, to give my client immunity for a day to go talk to the family, and he agreed. My client visited the family, apologized, answered all their questions, and together they turned the usual scenario of these cases upside down. When we went to court and resolved this case, everybody hugged beforehand, and everybody sat on the same side of the courtroom together. My client was an Iraq veteran who wanted to go back for another tour. He got a stay of his sentence and did not lose his license under the stipulation that he returned to Iraq, which he did.

Speeter believes that allowing people to talk to each other, to make room for apologies and connection and forgiveness, serves everyone best. "The only way to cut through the guilt, resentment, and other emotions that offenders, victims, and their families experience," he said, "is to promote understanding, which is another word for forgiveness."[113] Most of us associate forgiveness with condoning someone's behavior, but Bob describes it as a two-way street of understanding that brings resolution and emotional healing. I know that Michael Vang's experience in reaching out to David Riggs' parents with an apology was a powerful moment of healing in his life. Bob's ideas about bringing more of this into the court system give us a lot of food for thought.

* * *

It takes time for people to understand the risks of behavior that has become the norm. And when people start to take those risks seriously, it takes time for the law to catch up with society's attitudes. How much longer would it have taken automakers to install safety belts if Nader had not exposed the industry's deliberate safety negligence in his book? How many more tens of thousands of people would be killed by drunk drivers each year if MADD had not spent decades fighting for laws? Now it is our turn to fight for greater public awareness about distraction and tougher distraction laws. I am proud of the work of lawmakers like Senator Klobuchar who are committed to writing and passing anti-distraction legislation in Washington, and I am certain they will continue to fight the good fight for as long as it takes. The senator believes that it is everyone's responsibility to be proactive about ending distraction. "At the end of the day," she said, "it's up to all of us—from legislators to individual drivers and passengers—to do all we can to stop this dangerous practice."[114]

For Col. Matt Langer of the Minnesota State Patrol, the solution to distracted driving is just common sense. He believes we shouldn't even need a law because common sense should dictate what we're doing. "The perfect solution is people driving down the road having enough respect for other people that they pay attention," Langer said. "It's just that simple. I respect the kids playing ball, the pedestrians, and the other drivers. I respect other people enough that I'm going to take driving this potential killing machine down the road seriously. I'm going to pay attention."

Chapter 7

Changing Hearts and Minds: "Learning" Our Way Out of Distraction

> "We are collectively practicing distracted living."
> —Paul Aasen, President, Minnesota Safety Council

Now that you know the facts about the high risks of driving distracted and have heard real-life stories about how one split second of distraction can injure or kill, are you convinced? Will you turn off your phone or toss it into the glove compartment next time you get into your car or truck? Every driver's education instructor, safety agency, researcher, foundation, and individual committed to wiping out distracted driving hopes that their message compels you to do just that.

As strong as these messages may be (including the 'big' message of devoting an entire book to distraction), there are at least two huge forces working against the 'changing hearts and minds' approach. First, everything in our culture says that technology is good, interacting with technology anywhere and everywhere is normal, and technology is saving us—even in the car. The most blatant expression of this mindset that I have seen is Chevrolet's tagline about its hands-free system and text message alerts:

"Life doesn't stop when you're driving."[115]

The automaker may as well be saying, "Don't stop posting to Facebook, doing your banking, shopping, looking for a job, watching movies, playing video games, reading the news, checking the weather, texting, or talking on the phone just because you're driving. Life goes on behind the wheel!"

Could Chevrolet state anything more misleading? In truth, interacting with any kind of technology while driving raises the chance that life *will* stop. But with positive reinforcement like Chevy's marketing message, it is no wonder that so many drivers don't hesitate to do any of the above activities, regardless of knowing the facts and the law.

The second enormous challenge facing the educational approach is all in our heads. Once we hear something that we believe to be true, but later learn is false (turning the original information into misinformation), we tend to keep believing it is true anyway. Psychologists call this the 'continued influence effect.' Not only do we resist changing our mind, but our belief in that falsehood keeps getting stronger the more we hear the misinformation. The only way to shift out of this false belief is to receive equally strong retractions, or 'corrected' information. As one research study stated, "If misinformation is encoded [into memory] strongly, the level of continued influence will significantly increase, unless the misinformation is also retracted strongly."[116]

Many examples of this show up when a big news story catches the public's interest and is later corrected—much of the public perception stays with the original version. By the time the corrections are made, it is too late. All the excitement and attention paid to the initial story has made its mark in our memory banks, and not even the most clearly presented facts will change our mind:

> To use a notorious real-world example, the Bush administration purportedly made 935 false statements about the security risk posed by Iraq in the two years following 9/11. It is possible that the reiteration of this misinformation (i.e., that Iraq possessed WMDs) led to particularly powerful continued influence (e.g., the widespread continued belief in the existence of WMDs in Iraq).[117]

This quirk about human nature puts the pressure on anti-distraction groups to create strong messages and keep repeating them until they override misinformation like hands-free calling being 'safe.' If drivers keep using phones and electronics, eating, having conversations, grooming, and reaching around for things while driving, anti-distraction advocates must send them bigger and repeated messages about why they need to stop. Looking at the wide range of voices dedicated to sending these messages, I believe a movement has begun that will only get stronger. As part of the solution, along with laws and phone-blocking technology, education can counteract society's false messaging.

From national campaigns to in-school talks by ordinary people whose lives were changed by a distraction-caused crash, the message is getting through to audiences of all kinds. Let's take a look at what they are saying, and how they are saying it.

The National Wake-up Call

When Ray LaHood became the U.S. Secretary of Transportation in 2009, "not one person was talking about distracted driving," he said. Eighteen states had distracted driving laws at that time, but by the time he left the department in 2013, forty-four states had passed laws. "I am very proud that we were able to make this a national issue, a movement," he said.[118]

In his new position, he heard from many family members who had lost loved ones to distraction-induced crashes. "They told me that someone needed to step up and talk about this in a way that it had not been talked about," he said, "and it seemed very appropriate for the department and for me. We were responding to people's tragedies. I felt I had the platform, the bully pulpit, and I think we really got people's attention."[119]

The stories Secretary LaHood heard from visitors to his office were echoed by news he heard back home in Ohio. While at his home in Peoria one weekend, he read a newspaper article about a young woman driver who crashed into a tree and was killed. The report said she was texting and driving. "I did not know her," he said, "but she was someone from my home town, and that certainly had an impact."

Secretary LaHood was the first federal executive to launch a national conversation about distracted driving by calling it a "national epidemic." His department sponsored two Distracted Driving Summits in Washington, D.C., and since he knew about our foundation, he invited me to the first one in 2010. At that event, the secretary urged educators, legislators, and corporations to team up and develop educational programs, laws, and technology solutions to help institutionalize distraction-free driving across the country. I had an opportunity to speak to Secretary

LaHood privately about our work over breakfast one morning, and all the attendees learned about our foundation when Senator Klobuchar narrated Shreya's story in her keynote address. Seeing Secretary LaHood in action during that summit, with all his outspoken passion about combatting distracted driving, convinced me that this new movement had traction and support in the highest places.

At a press conference in 2011, LaHood announced the major strides his department had made in two short years:

> "We banned federal employees—a workforce of four million people—from texting while driving. We prohibited commercial truck and bus drivers from texting on the road—and proposed a ban on their cell phone use. And we continue running two pilot programs—one in Hartford, Connecticut and the other in Syracuse, New York—that test whether high-visibility enforcement and public-service announcements can change drivers' behaviors. The early data show that it can. Handheld cell phone use in the driver's seat has dropped 56 percent in Hartford and 38 percent in Syracuse—and texting behind the wheel declined 68 percent in Hartford and 42 percent in Syracuse.[120]

LaHood's public awareness campaigns included the "Faces of Distracted Driving" video series that shares the stories of families who have been affected by distraction-caused crashes. Under his leadership, the department also launched Distraction.gov, a website containing facts, figures, news, and more about distracted driving, and partnered with movie and TV studios, insurance companies, and others to inform viewers and customers about distracted driving.[121]

Another aspect of the secretary's education track was advising carmakers about specific infotainment design considerations that could help reduce crashes. "We knew that auto companies were going to keep putting a lot of tech into cars," LaHood said. "What we wanted to emphasize with them was that people shouldn't be able to receive texts or messages while they were driving. Many of the auto companies did adopt that."[122]

Secretary LaHood proposed the highest standards for eliminating distraction by phones. He ruffled feathers in the phone and software industries by insisting that the only safe phone in a car was a disabled phone. This led one reporter to ask, "So part of your ideal solution would be for drivers' phones to essentially be bricks while they're driving—completely disabled?"

"Absolutely," he said.[123]

State Programs

At the state level, traffic safety agencies educate the public through school programs, public service announcements, workshops, research about distracted-driving behaviors and trends, online information, and more. In Minnesota, the Office of Traffic Safety manages the state's Toward Zero Deaths (TZD) traffic safety initiative. This strategy focuses on four Es to reduce crashes: Education, Enforcement, Engineering, and Emergency Trauma Response. The education segment includes annual workshops throughout the state that help teachers, policymakers, engineers, emergency medical professionals, local law enforcement, and traffic safety advocates learn how to bring safety programs into their communities.

At least forty states have adopted the TZD model, and at the annual TZD conference, people share methods that work and don't work, so they can help each other build the best programs and avoid making the same mistakes. "It is taking off and it's working," said Minnesota Office of Traffic Safety Director Donna Berger. "We have done a significant reduction in traffic fatalities over the last decade, but there are always these new challenges coming up, like distracted driving." Overall, she said, fatalities are going down, "but we have this challenge with distracted driving, so we have to continue to work on it or those numbers are going to go up."[124]

Reaching people effectively, Berger said, seems to rely on getting personal, sharing real-world crash stories. Whether hearing speakers share these experiences or viewing them on videos, Facebook, or in Tweets, audiences are forced to contemplate the fact that it could just as easily happen to them. "We deal with a lot with numbers," Berger said, "and it's easy to get a little lost in that, so we've been trying to get it down to the stories. When people see the faces and hear the stories, they think, *That could be my family member. That could be me*. Hopefully that gives them the power to make better decisions."[125]

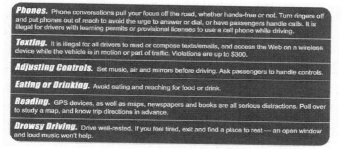

Phones. Phone conversations pull your focus off the road, whether hands-free or not. Turn ringers off and put phones out of reach to avoid the urge to answer or dial, or have passengers handle calls. It is illegal for drivers with learning permits or provisional licenses to use a cell phone while driving.

Texting. It is illegal for all drivers to read or compose texts/emails, and access the Web on a wireless device while the vehicle is in motion or part of traffic. Violations are up to $300.

Adjusting Controls. Set music, air and mirrors before driving. Ask passengers to handle controls.

Eating or Drinking. Avoid eating and reaching for food or drink.

Reading. GPS devices, as well as maps, newspapers and books are all serious distractions. Pull over to study a map, and know trip directions in advance.

Drowsy Driving. Drive well-rested. If you feel tired, exit and find a place to rest — an open window and loud music won't help.

Figure 10. A list of common distractions, from the Minnesota Office of Traffic Safety. This "Distracted Driving Card" also reminds drivers that "common distractions are the reasons inattentive driving accounts for one in four crashes in Minnesota." (dps.mn.com)

Minnesota Department of Public Safety Commissioner Ramona Dohman has spent her entire career in public safety, including ten years as the Chief of Police of Maple Grove, Minnesota. In her experience, the shock factor can have a strong impact in transforming teenagers' driving behavior.

A few years ago she witnessed how a shocking event altered her own daughter's behavior and attitude toward distracted driving:

> On February 20, 2012, I was taking our nineteen-year-old daughter back to North Dakota State University, and we drove by a crash that had occurred fifteen minutes earlier. Having pulled many dead bodies out of vehicles, I knew someone was dead or maybe everyone was dead because the car was demolished. We talked about that and said a prayer. By the time we got to NDSU, we learned the names of the four girls who had been killed in that crash. They were students at NDSU, and my daughter knew all four of them.
>
> The impact of being eyewitness to the scene and knowing the victims shocked her into a realization that no matter the cause, we have to do everything we can when we are behind the wheel to minimize the risk of distractions that could lead to what we saw. It was the shock factor that changed my daughter's attitude about distracted driving forever. She used to set her purse, with her phone inside, on the front seat. Now I see her put her purse in the back seat before she drives off.[126]

When she was a police chief, Commissioner Dohman used an in-class shock-factor approach that also made an impact. The teen driving program included an activity in which the students wrote an obituary-type letter to their parents, as if they were dead after a crash. There was dead silence, tears, and some outcries of "Bull----, I'm not going to do this," probably because they couldn't bear to do it. "The overall sentiment was, 'This is real; this could actually happen and I never thought about this before,'" Dohman said. "They think they are invincible at that age, but they are not. It really brought that to life."[127]

In many states, chapters of the National Safety Council offer driver's training and courses for many types of drivers, including people who drive for a living, like bus drivers, and specific age groups, such as mature drivers. Taking a driving course to simply improve skills, get a discount on an insurance premium, or satisfy a court-ordered requirement after a violation, can help drivers of all ages gain a stronger focus on driving without distractions.

The Minnesota Safety Council is also involved in recruiting new companies into the Minnesota Network of Employers for Traffic Safety (NETS). Part of the national non-profit organization Employers for Traffic Safety, Minnesota NETS helps company leaders write safety policies and education programs for employees. The National Safety Council recognizes exceptional leadership in creating safe working environments, and in 2014 it awarded its Green Cross for Safety Medal to Owens Corning. In addition to workplace safety, Owens Corning had launched a policy that banned cell phone use for employees while driving to conduct company business. Before announcing the plan to employees, CEO Michael Thaman tested the idea by driving phone-free for ninety days, and found that it did not affect his productivity. "To have the CEO get up in the [company] town hall and say that he spent the last ninety days without using his cell phone while driving, without it impacting his job, was a very powerful statement and demonstrated to all employees that it was possible," said the company's communications director.[128]

Paul Aasen, president of the Minnesota Safety Council, believes that education matters in reducing distracted driving because "you can't enforce your way to compliance" of the law. "However, even education has its limits," he said, "because it all comes down to a person's choice."[129]

Making wise choices in the driver's seat is more challenging than ever because our lives revolve around our personal devices. Aasen reflected on a story about a restaurant in New York City that hired a consultant to investigate why they were getting more and more complaints about the food and service. The investigator found that many of the customers pulled out their cell phones as soon as they were seated, ignored the menus while they toyed with their smartphones, and then complained that the waiters were slow. Once they got their food, they took pictures of it, let it get cold, and then complained about that. Spending time on the smartphone gave them a bizarre sense of stopped time, as if everything around them stood still while they were preoccupied. They missed the passage of time and events.[130]

"The moral of the story," Aasen said, "is that we are collectively practicing distracted living."[131]

Foundations

One of the biggest surprises Rekha and I encountered in our 2014 Raksha Walk was the appearance of a woman who traveled all the way from Texas to Minnesota to take part in the event. Jennifer Zamora-Jameson was eager to see what we were doing because she was developing her own foundation to combat distracted driving. We soon learned that her call to action came in the wake of personal tragedy.

Jennifer lost her husband, Javier Zamora, who was an Iraq War veteran, in 2007. He came home from the war in one piece and was killed on a U.S. highway by a distracted driver. The day he was killed, he was driving with their daughter to go school shopping:

> They were on a two-lane highway. A 19-year-old driver with a two-year-old child and two

> male adults in the vehicle with her were driving in the opposite direction. The driver was reaching behind her seat—she initially said it was for her phone, but she changed her story later and said it was something for her baby—but either way she lost control of her vehicle and hit Javier's car at sixty miles per hour. It ejected Javier out of the car and he died on the helicopter flight to the trauma center.[132]

The irony of the location of Javier's death was not lost on Jennifer, since he had survived a combat tour in Iraq as a helicopter door gunner. And she could never have anticipated the devastating repercussions the crash would bring:

> I attended my first Raksha Walk in August 2014. I met Vijay and Rekha and fell in love with them instantly, as everyone does. Right after I got home from that Minnesota visit, my 22-year-old daughter, who was involved in the car crash that took her dad's life, took her own life.

Maxine had survived her dad's crash with only a scratch on her nose. She always told us she didn't remember anything, but after she passed and I retrieved her diary I realized that not only did she remember it, but she remembered it in every detail. It affected her emotionally and mentally, and she struggled with that.[133]

Jennifer is now the Director of Policy and Advocacy for Stop Distractions, a national organization dedicated to raising awareness about distracted driving. She absorbed her own organization into that and continues to tell her story at conferences and through the websites she created in memory of Javier, "Decide to Drive," and Maxine, "Live to the Max." On the latter site, Jennifer focuses on the mental health side of distracted driving and helping survivors cope with it "so no one else has to live through the double tragedy that I've had to go through."[134]

Although she enjoys the educational facets of her advocacy work, Jennifer's passion is the legislative side because she sees a slow but certain path to change. The social and judicial perspective of distracted driving today is where MADD was thirty years ago, she said. "Taking a life through negligence, which is what driving while distracted is to me, should be just as punishable as if you were driving drunk and taking a life. The stigma, the punishment, the taboo of it—we need to be in the same mental and judicial place, because it is the same type of crime."[135]

Education is the heartbeat of the Casey Feldman Memorial Foundation and its main project, EndDD. org. Joel Feldman and his wife, Dianne Anderson, created the foundation after their 21-year-old daughter, Casey, was killed by a distracted driver in 2009. Casey was about to enter her senior year at

Fordham University in New York City, where she was studying communications and media studies. She died on a clear day in July while walking to her summer job as a waitress in New Jersey. Nearly at the end of a crosswalk in an intersection with four-way stop signs, she was struck by a van driven by a 58-year-old man who was reaching for his GPS and holding an iced tea. He said he never saw her.

Three months later, Joel was grief stricken and lost. Out walking the dog one morning, he wondered how life could ever be the same for his wife, his son, and his family. Unexpectedly, his attention changed. "It was cool and crisp," he said. "The grass was kind of frosted over, crunching a little bit when I walked over it. It was a sensory moment—the sun was coming up, the geese were flying overhead, the lighting was incredible. All of a sudden something came over me. I thought, *It's awful, but it can be better and it's going to be better and I have to do something so that Casey's life and death have meaning.*[136]

Joel began talking to school kids about distracted driving. When he tried to find a science-backed presentation about distracted driving to enhance his talks he could not find one, so he did his own research and developed his own. An attorney by day, he then entered night school to earn a master's degree in counseling because he knew the solution was to change drivers' behavior. As he learned more about the science of distraction, he teamed up with experts from the Children's Hospital of Philadelphia to expand his presentation into a state-of-the-art, research-backed awareness program. That project, thanks to the seven hundred trained volunteers (many of them lawyers) who present it across the country, has now reached over 275,000 students and adults.

At age sixty, Joel began running to raise awareness about distracted driving. He is optimistic about the future because the positive feedback and emails that come in after the presentations prove that the message is getting through—people are changing their habits and putting away their phones. He is also optimistic about the potential of the next generation to turn this crisis around. "There are a lot of folks out there who say the millennials are the most caring generation, the most caring people in the world," he said. "If you can reach out to them and harness all that energy and caring, how can you not be optimistic?"[137]

Jon Cummings founded Minnesotans for Safe Driving (MSD) in 2000 after many years of helping victims of drunk-driving crashes connect with the resources they needed. Jon and his co-founder, long-time victim advocate Nancy Johnson, set up the non-profit organization to expand their services to victims of all types of crashes, including those caused by distracted driving. In addition to helping victims, the mission of MSD is to change drivers' behavior by educating the public to the dangers of drunk driving and distracted driving.

A central part of MSD's work is holding Victim Impact Panels, where victims, offenders, medical workers, and law enforcement officers speak to crash offenders and the public about the real-world consequences of distracted driving. They also speak at schools, give death notification and sensitivity training to officials who must announce crash deaths to families, and lobby for traffic safety laws at the Minnesota legislature.

Jon's passion for education and advocacy began after his 23-year-old son, Phillip, was killed by a drunk driver. Phillip had just finished his night shift at a restaurant in Plymouth, Minnesota, and picked up his friend, Jeff, to set out for Mystic Lake Casino in Prior Lake. They got onto I-494, and all Jeff remembered after that was a flash of light. When he woke up, he was covered in broken glass and heard Phillip drowning in his own blood. "He sat there and held Phillip until he bled to death," Jon said. "Jeff has never been the same since."[138]

The driver who caused the crash had been drinking on the golf course all day and in a bar all night. He got lost on the freeway, turned into the wrong lane, and crashed head-on into Phillip's car. The driver survived and never took responsibility for the crash, causing a year of legal nightmares for Jon and his family. In the end, the offender was sentenced to five years in prison. Jon has been working in restorative justice ever since, helping victims and offenders restore their lives after a crash.

In MSD's Impact Panel meetings, people convicted of distracted or drunk driving are ordered by the court to listen to victims and offenders whose lives are forever changed by this behavior. "They tell the truth," Jon said. "'We're no different than you, and if this can happen to us, use your heads.' We're just trying to get people to look at this from a different angle."[139]

Building on Brain Science: Distraction-free Clubs for Teenagers

Teen driving behaviors are intriguing. These young drivers are intelligent, alert, and highly capable of handling difficult challenges while playing sports. Some excel in band, speech, or other activities and even manage to keep up their grades while holding down part-time jobs. Despite all that, at times they are very unpredictable. Most of us attribute that to typical teenage behavior. Parents expect that to change as they grow up, but I find it hard to accept that logic. I am an analytical thinker and have tried to dig deeper into the process of teen decision-making.

I remember times in my teen years when I found it difficult to challenge the norm while in the midst of my peers. Sometimes it was to protect my ego, and other times to avoid hurting a dear friend. I would rather go with the flow than act on my personal wishes. Sometimes when a friend was dismissive of things I loved, I just followed suit because everyone else around us agreed with the friend. Adapting my behavior to the group, or bending to social influence or peer pressure, was—and still is—typical teen behavior.

In my search for answers about how teens think I came upon the work of British scientist Sarah-Jayne Blakemore, whom I introduced in Chapter 5. A researcher and professor at University College London, Blakemore studies the development of social cognition and executive function in the developing adolescent brain. Her research is giving us a new vision of brain development throughout our lifespan:

> The idea that the brain is somehow fixed in early childhood, which was an idea that was very strongly believed up until fairly recently, is completely wrong. There's no evidence that the brain is somehow set and can't change after early childhood. In fact, it goes through this very large development throughout adolescence and right into the twenties and thirties, and even after that it's plastic forever; the plasticity is a baseline state, no

matter how old you are. That has implications for things like intervention programs and educational programs for teenagers.[140]

Doctor Blakemore states that teenagers are more prone to accidents and unintended actions that turn into tragedies. Generally such accidents are caused by the risk-taking behaviors rampant among teenagers. Her premise is that the teen years are filled with heightened self-consciousness and burdened with peer pressure with a strong desire for peer approval. They seem to get hung up on being 'cool.' According to Blakemore, teenagers are "driven to develop a sense of self and self-identity, and especially a sense of who they are, how they're seen by other people, in particular their peers." This explains, from an evolutionary point of view, the increased drive to take risks. A teenager feels compelled to "move away from the relative security of your family and your parents, and take risks by discovering things for yourself in the outside world."[141]

Research conducted by B. J. Casey of Cornell University reports similar results. One study identifies the role that environmental conditions play in influencing decision-making among teens. We often find teenagers making very quick, accurate judgments and decisions on their own in situations where they have time to think before acting. However, when they have to make decisions in the heat of the moment, their choices are often influenced by external factors, such as knowing they are being watched by their friends. Based on this connection between biology and peer pressure, it is easier to understand why teenagers are prone to performing risky activities while driving.

But I also see a silver lining there. If teens are easily influenced by risky/bad behaviors, they may be equally influenced by friends who encourage 'good' behavior. Teenagers may join a volunteer group because their friends are doing it, or try to improve their grades because the social group they belong to believes that getting good grades is important. In fact, friends often encourage each other to study, try out for sports, or follow new artistic interests. I will never forget the positive influence I received from a very good friend during my college days. He got me hooked on the Advaita philosophy of a fourteenth-century Indian sage. At the same time, two other friends in New Delhi got me entrenched in India's classical music tradition. I also had very good friends who scoffed at philosophy and classical music as things that only 'old people' did. But the others had more influence me, and I thank them every day.

Peer influence can lead teens to engage in new activities that help build strong pathways in the brain. When these activities include reinforcing safer driving behavior, teenagers may decide that tossing the cell phone in the back seat before getting behind the wheel is the cool thing to do. Since peer-based methods may be very effective in fighting distracted-driving behavior among teens, it makes sense to develop new approaches based on peer influence. Instead of relying on lectures from parents, we may have good results by establishing peer-led groups/clubs in high schools to spread the message of distraction-free driving. This is what our foundation began to do in 2015.

At the start of the new school year we established the first group of Distraction-free Driving Clubs at three Minnesota high schools. As of this writing these clubs are still in their first year. Two student leaders run each club with a faculty member serving as the club counselor for administrative oversight. Membership is open to all grades, from freshmen to seniors, and each club chooses the projects they want to run. We set up guidelines, however, so that each project has measurable performance criteria that we can assess. This will allow us to determine how effective the projects are from year to year. We are also exploring collaborations with experts from the academic and technical fields to develop credible metrics for measuring the overall success of these clubs.

What would success look like in these clubs? I categorized a vision of success on two levels, one for the foundation and one for the students. With a few variables intact, this plan is a measuring tool for the club's effectiveness:

1. Foundation Success Criteria:

   a. Create a "Distraction Craving Index" for different types of distractions with a risk assigned to each one. This then extends to a Consolidated Distraction Craving Index

   b. Grow the number of clubs in Minnesota high schools to a specified rate

   c. Create a mechanism to track changes in driving behaviors among club members

   d. Keep count of non-club members influenced by club members

   e. Count the number of new initiatives started in a calendar year

2. Club Success Criteria:

   f. Create yearly targets for a reduction in the Craving Index at each club

   g. Target and measure member growth at each club

   h. Design new incentives to encourage better driving behaviors

i. Launch a club-to-club competition on reducing the Craving Index to win awards and recognition

Activities in the clubs include meetings with safety experts from the government, academic community, and private industry to learn about tools and techniques that may instill distraction-free driving practices. All club members serve as peer advocates to spread the message to the whole student body at their schools.

The current clubs are pilot programs, models for an approach that we hope proves to be effective. When we can establish that, we plan to replicate them in schools across Minnesota and beyond.

Finding Our "Why"

Almost every person I know who advocates for distraction-free driving through an agency, foundation, or other group recognizes from experience that personal stories reach audiences at the deepest level. The impact of these presentations brings us back to the psychological challenge mentioned earlier. Advertising and the culture at large have given us a false belief about the 'safety' of talking or texting hands-free. Perhaps emotional, real-life stories will 'overwrite' these beliefs with equally or more powerful messages about distraction and inattention blindness. This also ties in with Simon Sinek's concept of the power of 'why'—getting to the meaningful, why-it-matters core of a message so that it will resonate in the limbic center of the brain.[142] The limbic brain is the emotional center responsible for our feelings of trust, our decision-making, and our behavior. The brutally honest stories that people tell about the consequences of distraction tap into that part of the brain and may hold the key to 'learning' our way out of the distraction epidemic.

Many of the safety experts and advocates I have met agree that the only real-world solution to distracted driving is a combination of all three areas: technology, laws, and education. Matt Richtel, the Pulitzer Prize-winning journalist and author of *A Deadly Wandering*, is both discouraged and optimistic about the future of distraction. "For all the public awareness and all the laws, the behavior is going up, not down," he said. "That is a remarkable thing because it flies in the face of everything we know about how you curb behavior from drunk driving to safety belts."[143] At the same time, like Joel Feldman, Matt puts a lot of faith in the next generation:

> An encouraging thing is that you have seen more people take up the mantle of this as a serious topic. I think to the extent that you can get young people engaged it is theoretically encouraging because sometimes it is generational. Your kids will say, 'Hey, Dad,

put on your seatbelt.' They can become change agents. The more we talk about this, the more young people will get involved.[144]

Youth education projects throughout the country, run by government agencies, non-profits, and individuals, including our foundation's high-school clubs, are working hard to create that involvement and send young change agents out into the world to build a safer future.

Chapter 8

We Can Change the World

"Slow down everyone
You're moving too fast
Frames can't catch you when
You're moving like that."
—from "Inaudible Melodies," Jack Johnson

Shreya loved the music of American singer-songwriter Jack Jackson. She related to the laid-back style of this surfer-turned-musician whose creativity and success is only matched by his generosity. Jackson, who puts his passion for ecology and sustainability into his own foundations, walks his talk, just as Shreya did. Shreya loved people, loved being with and caring for them. The center of her life was expressing love and friendship in any way she could, from bringing friends together for evenings in our living room to acting as a gentle referee when her friends squabbled. Shreya lived out Jackson's philosophy of slowing down, living a more natural life, putting a priority on love, and connecting. That message now flows through the foundation that bears her name.

This book has shared the real-life experiences, facts and figures, and possible solutions that make up the story of the distracted driving epidemic. The Shreya R. Dixit Memorial Foundation is committed to moving this story toward happier endings than tragic ones. It is done through public talks and events, annual walks, high-school clubs, media interviews, original research, this book, and most of all, our rock-solid faith in people. We believe that people have a stronger instinct to act out of respect for others than out of selfishness. We believe that once people understand the deadly risks of distracted driving they will choose to do the right thing. We believe that people care about each other, even the strangers driving along the road with them, more than they care about satisfying a fleeting impulse to look at or pick up the phone, reach out for things in the car, or perform any activity that diverts from the primary task of driving. These beliefs keep us going.

Our dangerous behavior behind the wheel can change dramatically when we take responsibility for our actions. Movements like Mothers Against Drunk

Driving prove this. MADD teaches us that people change their behavior when they understand that the *act* of drinking and driving is the evil, not the *people* who do the act. Because of MADD, drunk driving is not only outlawed, but is also a deep-seated cultural taboo. One day, distracted driving will be just as taboo. Teenagers will look back at this time and cry out to their parents, "What?! You talked on your phone while you drove? You texted behind the wheel? What were you—crazy?!"

Anyone can make a mistake because part of the American Dream is freedom of choice. In previous pages we have witnessed how good, ordinary people have freely made a bad choice and caused suffering and, in extreme cases, a fatality. But attitudes are changing and the future may look very different. When people feel good about freely making a choice to not be distracted, shutting down the distractions in the car will become second nature. They will drive safely. Lives will be saved. And all those results will be our reward.

A Call to Action

Change happens through cooperation and collaboration. Our foundation is expanding its network of partners and creating a bold new vision of strong ties with the businesses that have a direct impact on the distracted driving epidemic. Strong relationships with public and private driver education programs, state and federal traffic safety departments/ agencies, and academic research institutions are just the beginning. We look forward to forging alliances with insurance companies, phone manufacturers, electronic communication device makers, and the auto industry to turn distraction into a thing of the past.

Only by working together can we create new habits that will make our roads safer. The blueprint will contain new policies, new priorities, and new actions laser-focused on abolishing distraction.

Insurance Companies

Auto insurance companies have a huge stake in distracted driving, and they know that teen drivers are the riskiest drivers on the road. Our foundation can help change their customers' behavior by suggesting how to integrate the programs from our high-school clubs into their training and messaging projects. What works for us in high schools can translate into their approaches, and together we can build strong national programs that stop distraction. Insurance companies are working toward solutions, such as the discounts in car insurance rates that State Farm makes available in some states for those who complete the Steer Clear® program (watch a video, make a pledge, discuss the pledge with an agent, etc.), and GEICO's "Tips to Avoid Distracted Driving" posted on its website.

These are steps in the right direction, but they are just first steps. And the upward trend of car crashes on American roads is having an impact on insurance company's profits, which may be the biggest wakeup call to motivate the industry to take bigger steps. In September 2015 GEICO's owner, billionaire Warren Buffet, told the *Wall Street Journal* that more technology in cars is not making roads safer. Commenting on the increase in accidents that is affecting GEICO's bottom line, Buffet said, "If cars are better—and they clearly are—drivers must be worse."[145] When Buffet talks, his businesses—and businesses all over the world—listen, and his comments about bad driver behavior may be a major turning point in the insurance industry's approach to distracted driving. Car insurance companies have a responsibility *and* a profit incentive to do everything in their power to solve the distraction epidemic.

We will do everything we can to be part of that solution.

Phone Manufacturers and Providers

Like the insurance industry, phone companies continue to develop campaigns to raise awareness about the dangers of distracted driving. As explored in Chapter 3, they are also creating apps to inhibit calling and texting while driving, such as AT&T's DriveMode and Sprint's Drive First. In spite of these excellent efforts, however, crash rates are rising and

1 in 5 drivers of all ages admits to surfing the web while driving. Working alone, phone makers and carriers are not getting the job done.

Our foundation believes that these industries must take responsibility for the deadly risks that their devices create when their customers bring them into a vehicle. We will call for a black-box label to be fixed to cell phones, tablets, and other portable devices, as well as phone bills, to warn users that these devices are deadly when used while driving. Just as the Food and Drug Administration required drug and tobacco companies to warn about the dangers of their products, a national policy must be put in place that demands that phones and other devices come with a powerful warning about the deadly risk of using the product while driving. The facts about the deadly risks are clear, with years of research to back them up. Phone companies will be one step closer to giving their customers a fighting chance to stay alive on the road if they create a clear and dire warning about their products.

Consider the impact that the following labels would have if every cell phone and phone bill carried them:

WARNING
THIS PRODUCT IS ADDICTIVE

WARNING
DRIVING WHILE TEXTING
IS MORE DANGEROUS
THAN DRIVING DRUNK

The Auto Industry

In the above-mentioned article about GEICO, Warren Buffet said that cars are 'better.' With all due respect to Mr. Buffet, he was wrong. More technology does not equal more safety. As discussed in Chapter 2, one of the main reasons that the distraction epidemic is out of control is that we are receiving a message from the car companies and the entire tech world that hands-free calling and touch displays on the dash are safe. They are not. Distraction is distraction, as so clearly described by the scientists who have contributed to this book.

The Distraction Index

When I start thinking about buying a car, I do some simple research by checking out the ratings in *Consumer Reports*. It just makes sense to me to rely on this magazine's analyses of safety, comfort, reliability, gas mileage, and other factors to help me make a smart decision. Published by the Consumers Union, which was founded in 1936, *Consumer*

Reports never takes paid ads, so I feel confident that its ratings are not biased. Throughout its history, this magazine has given buyers an edge by revealing the sometimes shocking facts about car 'safety,' from seatbelts to rollover ratings.

The time has come for another ratings column in this important report: "The Mental Distraction Risk Index." Consumers have a right to be able to compare the distraction risks of the onboard technology among any given models of cars, trucks, vans, or SUVs. In fact, such a rating is needed for all electronic communication devices that may be used in motorized vehicles. We should expect our devices to come with up-front information about the safety risks involved if used when driving—information based on the facts about distraction. Bringing the facts into the mainstream will help tech-hungry young drivers as well as tech-savvy adults make smart decisions about safety.

Consumer Reports is most qualified to develop insightful criteria for these electronic devices and apps that target the fast-evolving markets of connected vehicles. Consumers turn to this journal for health and environment ratings of soaps, cereals, and detergents before buying them. Why wouldn't they do the same for electronic devices and apps?

We suggest a collaborative engagement approach in partnership with all stakeholders to develop a universally acceptable Mental Distraction Risk Index that will help consumers make intelligent buying decisions. Without the index, we are not aware of the high risks associated with technology that is marketed as the 'safe' and cutting-edge answer to 'distraction-free' driving. One example of this false messaging is the claim of Head Up Display (HUD) technology marketed for cars. This new technology, with roots in aviation, displays a screen across the bottom of the windshield. Texts, navigation, maps, social-media alerts, call information—all types of words and images that appear on a smartphone can now appear on the windshield.

One manufacturer of this technology boasts that it is "the safest and most intuitive way to make calls, use navigation, listen to music or access notifications without ever looking away from the road."[146] When using a navigation app, there is even a split screen with a second visual notification for an incoming call. *Brilliant.*

The so-called benefit claimed is that the driver need not look away from the front windshield; however, brain research has proven that if our eyes are focused on anything except the road, we are driving blind. The National Highway Traffic Safety Administration's anti-distraction guidelines recommend that automakers display *zero* characters from social media or text messages while the car is moving.[147] A mind focused on reading and interacting with words and images on the windshield is still a mind distracted from the road. Head Up Display technology is not a solution, but instead one more form of distraction that is being hyped as 'safe.'

The HUD technologies address visual distraction and ignore the risk of cognitive distraction, the dangers of which have been so clearly researched by scientists like David Strayer. That research teaches us that the root cause of distraction is inattention blindness, a state of mind in which the driver's mental activity is on something other than driving. Cognitive distractions are more threatening than visual distractions, such as poor visibility due to weather, or manual distractions like hitting an unexpected speed bump.

How does the HUD technology in the latest car models measure up to the facts about cognitive distraction? This is a question every consumer should ask. *Consumer Reports* could play a very important role by testing all tech devices and apps for cognitive distraction and offering the results in a Distraction Risk Index.

An easy-to-understand distraction index is one idea for combating the distracted-driving epidemic. Our foundation's work with teens in the Distraction-Free-Driving Clubs in Minnesota high schools and with experts at the University of Minnesota to help develop innovative programs are more ways that we hope to make a difference.

Change a Life, Change the World

In Chapter 3, I introduced Michael Vang, the nineteen-year-old whose three-second distraction caused a crash that killed his friend, David. When I took on the assignment of overseeing Michael's one hundred hours of community service with the foundation, it was difficult at first. I was hounded by the thought that I would see in Michael the offender in Shreya's crash. But I stayed with the challenge by reminding myself about why I was doing it. It was important for me to recognize his inner pain of carrying the guilt for the rest of his life. That opened up the door of empathy and I started to envision a positive end result. I set a goal of helping Michael manage and even heal his guilt, move on with his life, and be a powerful messenger about distraction-free driving.

After bringing Michael to a few of our panel presentations at high schools and other venues, I convinced him to participate in our next panel and tell his story. As I hoped, he felt better after that first talk. He had bared his soul and, maybe, persuaded the audience to put their phones away when they got behind the wheel.

For several months Michael joined me at teen panels, driver education schools, and our 2015

Raksha Walk, where he told his story and how it impacted him and the victim's family and friends. Speaking at the events never got easier emotionally, but he did gain more confidence each time. Each time he gave his talk he admitted that looking at his phone was an irresponsible act. He took responsibility for his actions and grew stronger as a result. His talks were opportunities to rejoin society and be part of the solution.

Thanks to my years of grief therapy with Susan, I knew it would be helpful to encourage Michael to form a relationship with his friend who died in the crash. That would be a critical part of helping him process his experience and move out of paralyzing guilt into a life with purpose. Michael described his experience with the foundation as a turnaround in his life:

> Before working with the foundation it was really hard for me. I was in a shell. I didn't know what to do. Every day passed and I was just lying to myself, telling myself I would be OK. If you don't take the negative energy and make something positive out of it, it's always going to haunt you. I had to do something about it. I had to redeem myself.

> When I reached out to Vijay, he comforted me. He told me that the trauma would never completely go away, but that I could learn how to turn it into something positive. He did some counseling with me. He encouraged me to be a speaker, to go out to schools, to talk

to young people, to promote the message. At first I didn't think it would benefit me, because we're different people. But coming out to the walks, seeing new faces, and being a speaker made me strong, and that really helped me. Vijay really pushed me to do all that, and I'm glad he did.

Now I see David as a brother. I feel like he's been a big part of my life and made me a stronger person. When I give a talk, I feel like David is with me.

I also believed Michael would benefit from reaching out to David's family with an apology. I told him it was very important that he get closure, and that if the family accepted his apology his pain would be tremendously reduced.

Such an act would undoubtedly have a healing effect on the victim family, too. Michael put a lot of thought into his two-page, hand-written letter to David's family. In the Twin Cities television news segment about distracted driving that featured our foundation and the Riggs family, David's mother, Peggy Riggs, talked about her response to Michael's letter:

I appreciate that he thinks about David every day. I want him to because I think it's going to make him a better person. And I think the most important thing is not that *we* can forgive him, but that he needs to forgive himself. And I know that's what David would want.[148]

I believe Michael's victim family may have found some peace after receiving his apology letter. The remorse Michael communicated was genuine, in my view, and I believe they felt it. There will never be complete closure; the deep feeling of loss will not go away. But the family did get the opportunity to interact with Michael through his heartfelt written words, and that connection is meaningful for all of them.

Opening doors of communication and healing were not the only impacts that came from working with Michael. His transformation from an incoherent, guilt-ridden offender to a proactive advocate far exceeded his probation officer's expectations. She believed this worked out better for the court system as well as the offender, and most important of all, offered some comfort to the victim family. Perhaps our approach planted some seeds for similar approaches that the system may suggest in future cases.

* * *

My year with Michael was equally transforming for me. The process gave me an opportunity to show empathy, care, and kindness to someone who had shattered a family, just as mine had been shattered. Before working with Michael, I did not think I was capable of that. But we helped each other bring more harmony to our lives. Nothing we do will bring back

Shreya, David, or any of the 60 people who are killed in distraction-affected crashes in Minnesota every year, but I believe our work is saving future lives.

November 1, 2016, will mark nine years since the crash that took Shreya's life. We have done the best we can to move from a grief-stricken family to a force for positive change. And through it all Shreya has reached out to us through countless signs and so-called coincidences. A year ago on November 1, our daughter Nayha was signing in for her appointment at a hair salon in San Francisco. The name on the line above hers on the schedule sheet was… "Shreya."

May all your journeys be safe.

AUM saha navavatu,
saha nau bhunaktu.
Saha veeryam karvaavahai.
Tejasvi naa vadhita mastu.

Let us together be protected and let us together be nourished by God's blessings.
Let us together join our mental forces in strength for the benefit of humanity.
Let our efforts at learning be luminous and filled with joy, and endowed with the force of purpose.

APPENDIX

Resources about Distracted Driving

Websites

Government Sites

Centers for Disease Control and Prevention (also
contains a teen driving page): www.cdc.gov/
motorvehiclesafety/distracted_driving/

Distracted Driving Laws, Governors Highway
Safety Association: ghsa.org/html/stateinfo/
laws/cellphone_laws.html

Minnesota Department of Public Safety, Office of
Traffic Safety (includes fact sheets, "Teen
Driver Road Rules" brochure, etc.): dps.
mn.gov/divisions/ots

National Highway Traffic Safety Administration,
Distraction: nhtsa.gov/Research/
Crash+Avoidance/Distraction

National Safety Council: www.nsc.org

Safer Car (official U.S. government list of vehicle
safety ratings): safercar.gov

Official U.S. Government Website for Distracted
Driving: distraction.gov

Foundations & Organizations

AAA Foundation for Traffic Safety:
AAAfoundation.org

AAA Minneapolis: Minneapolis.aaa.com

Blog for Parents of Teen Drivers: www.
fromreidsdad.org

Decide2drive (Jennifer Zamora-Jameson): www.
decide2drive.org

Distracted Driving Foundation: www.ddfn.org

End Distracted Driving (Casey Feldman
Foundation): www.enddd.org/

Hang Up and Drive (Jacy Good): www.
hangupanddrive.com

Lifesavers Conference (traffic safety professionals):
lifesaversconference.org

Minnesota Safety Council: www.
minnesotasafetycouncil.org

Minnesotans for Safe Driving: mnsafedriving.com

Mothers Against Drunk Driving (MADD): www.
madd.org

Mourning Parents Act: mourningparentsact.org

National Organizations for Youth Safety: www.
noys.org

People Against Distracted Driving (Nikki Kellenyi
Foundation), www.padd.org

Shreya R. Dixit Memorial Foundation: shreyadixit.org

Stay Alive . . . Just Drive: www.sajd.org/sajd/about-sajd

Students Against Destructive Decisions: www.sadd.org

Training

Adaptive Massive Open Online Course (aMOOC)
Free eTraining Tool: shreyadixit.org/free-
distraction-free-driver-etrainer/

Children's Hospital of Philadelphia, Training Tools:
teendriversource.org

Dakota County Technical College: www.dctc.edu

Gauging Your Distraction (*New York Times*
interactive game): www.nytimes.com/
interactive/2009/07/19/technology/20090719-
driving-game.html

Impact Teen Drivers: impactteendrivers.org

Minnesota Highway Safety & Research Center:
www.mnsafetycenter.org

Industry

Apple CarPlay: www.apple.com/ios/carplay/

AT&T DriveMode: www.att.com/gen/press-
room?pid=23185

Cellcontrol: www.cellcontrol.com

DriveSafe Mode: drivesafemode.com/

Google AndroidAuto: www.android.com/auto/

It Can Wait: www.itcanwait.com/all

Liberty Mutual Insurance: libertymutual.com/
teendriving

Sprint Drive First: sprint-drivefirst.safely.com/

State Farm Insurance Teen Driver Safety:
teendriving.statefarm.com

T-Mobile DriveSmart: support.t-mobile.com/docs/
DOC-2374

Toyota TeenDrive 365: toyota.com/teendrive365/

Verizon SafelyGo: www.safely.com/products/go/

Research Labs

University of Minnesota HumanFirst Laboratory:
www.humanfirst.umn.edu/index.html

Virginia Tech Transportation Institute Center for
Automotive Safety Research: www.vtti.
vt.edu/index.html

Books

Matt Richtel, *A Deadly Wandering: A Tale of Tragedy and Redemption in the Age of Attention*, HarperCollins, 2014.

Tim Hollister, *His Father Still: A Parenting Memoir*, Argo-Navis, 2015.

Tim Hollister, *Not So Fast: Parenting Your Teen Through the Dangers of Driving*, Chicago Review Press, 2013.

Videos

"Defeat Distracted Driving," shreyadixit.org

EDU Film Festival: vimeo.com/edufilmfest

"In a Split Second" documentary, shreyadixit.org

"Lawyer Teen-Parent Rules," dps.mn.gov

"Parents are the Key to Safe Drivers," www.cdc.gov

"Point of Impact," dps.mn.gov

"Texting While Driving," AT&T: www.youtube.com/watch?v=dht-Vy25jPs

The Faces of Distracted Driving: www.distraction.gov/experience-the-stories/index.html

Interviewees

Paul Aasen
Donna Berger
Jon Cummings
Kristen Bauer
Nayha Dixit
Rekha Dixit
Ramona Dohman
Frank Douma
Barbara Eisenmenger
Joel Feldman
Jacy Good
Deborah Hersman
Nancy Johnson
Amy Klobuchar
Art Kosieradzki
Ray LaHood
Matt Langer
Nichole Morris
Jake Nelson
Gordy Pehrson
Susan Reynolds
Matt Richtel
Mark Ritchie
Bridget Roby
Fran Roby
Tiffani Schweigart
Robert Speeter
David L. Strayer
Michael Vang
Chris Weber
Jennifer Zamora-Jameson

Endnotes

1   "Distracted Driving," Centers for Disease Control and Prevention, August 13, 2015, www.cdc.gov/

2   Javed Akhtar, lyrics "Do Pal," bollynook.com/en/lyrics/6396/do-pal.

3   Barbara Kingsolver, *High Tide in Tucson: Essays from Now or Never,* New York: HarperCollins, 1995.

4   Kate McCarthy, "Remembering Shreya," *Minneapolis Star-Tribune*, July 18, 2009.

5   Interview with Michael Vang, August 1, 2015

6   Interview with Mark Ritchie, July 27, 2015.

7   Lindsey Seavert, "Texting and Driving: Message Still Not Received," KARE11, www.kare11.com/story/traffic/2015/11/16/texting-and-driving-on-minnesota-roads-a-message-still-not-received/75907774/

8   "Distracted Driving 2013" and "Distracted Driving 2012," National Highway Traffic Safety Administration, Distraction.gov

9   Mary Madden, Amanda Lenhart, Maeve Duggan, Sandra Cortesi, and Urs Gasser, "Teens and Technology 2013," Pew Research Center, March 13, 2013, www.pewinternet.org/2013/03/13/teens-and-technology-2013/

10   David L. Strayer, Frank A. Drews, and Dennis J. Crouch, "A Comparison of the Cell Phone Driver and the Drunk Driver," *Human Factors,* Summer 2006, www.distraction.gov/downloads/pdfs/a-comparison-of-the-cell-phone-driver-and-the-drunk-driver.pdf

11   Distraction.gov, www.distraction.gov/stats-research-laws/facts-and-statistics.html

12   Distraction.gov

13   Distraction.gov

14   David L. Strayer, Frank A. Drews, and Dennis J. Crouch, "Fatal Distraction? A Comparison of the Cell-phone Driver and the Drunk Driver," University of Utah, www.psych.utah.edu/AppliedCognitionLab/DrivingAssessment2003.pdf

15   Interview with Chris Weber, October 1, 2015

16   "Shattered Dreams: Distracted Driving Changes Lives," www.youtube.com/watch?v=mKKw-Q1M80o

17   Interview with Chris Weber, October 1, 2015

18   Matt Richtel, "In Study, Texting Lifts Crash Risk by Large Margin," *New York Times*, July 27, 2009, www.nytimes.com/2009/07/28/technology/28texting.html

19   Distraction.gov

20   Telephone interview with David Strayer, April 24, 2015.

21   Telephone interview with David Strayer, April 24, 2015.

22   Telephone interview with David Strayer, April 24, 2015.

23   Telephone interview with David Strayer, April 24, 2015.

24   Donald L. Fisher and David L. Strayer, "Modeling Situation Awareness and Crash Risk," Annals of Advances in Automotive Medicine, March 2014, www.ncbi.nlm.nih.gov/pmc/articles/PMC4001668/

25   Interview with Tiffani Schweigart, September 15, 2015.

26   "Distracted Driving 2013"

27   "Distracted Driving 2013"

28   Interview with Jacy Good, August 21, 2015

29   Interview with Jacy Good, August 21, 2015

30   "Distracted Driving 2013" and "Distracted Driving 2012,"
        National Highway Traffic Safety Administration, Distraction.gov

31   "Distracted Driving 2013"

32   "2014 Traffic Safety Culture Index," AAA Foundation for
        Traffic Safety, January 2015, www.aaafoundation.org/sites/
        default/files/2014TSCIreport.pdf

33   Mike Rugani, "Minnesota Distracted Driving Survey,"
        presentation at the TZD Stakeholder Breakfast, January 6,
        2016.

34   "Driven to Distraction," American Psychological Association,
        www.apa.org/research/action/drive.aspx

35   Consumer Reports, "Auto Infotainment Systems 101," www.
        consumerreports.org.

36   David Strayer et al, "Measuring Cognitive Distraction in the
        Automobile, AAA Foundation for Traffic Safety, June 2013.

37   David Strayer et al, "Measuring Cognitive Distraction in the
        Automobile II: Assessing In-Vehicle Voice-Based Interactive
        Technologies," AAA Foundation for Traffic Safety, October
        2014.

38   National Highway Traffic Safety Administration, "U.S. DOT
        Releases Guidelines to Minimize In-Vehicle Distractions,"
        April 23, 2013, NHTSA.gov.

39   National Highway Traffic Safety Administration, April 23,
        2013.

40   "Welcome to the Infotainment Revolution," Consumer
        Reports, April 2015.

41   "Automakers Still Trying to Get Infotainment Systems Right,"
        National Public Radio, July 29, 2015.

42   "Sending and Receiving Text on Chevy MyLink," www.
        youtube.com/watch?v=FEupd-2shzY.

43   "Using Text Messaging with MyFord Touch," www.youtube.com/watch?v=0uP1ys6jl1k.

44   "Easiest Way to Use Text Messaging and Pairing with Cadillac CUE," www.youtube.com/watch?v=8PsHGSDM6K4

45   Gregory Fink, "A Wildly High Percentage Of Tesla Drivers Read The Drudge Report While Behind The Wheel," April 3, 2014, Huffingtonpost.com.

46   Strayer et al, "Measuring Cognitive Distraction in the Automobile III: A Comparison of Ten 2015 In-Vehicle Information Systems," AAA Foundation for Traffic Safety, October 2015.

47   Strayer et al, October 2015.

48   Sarah-Jayne Blakemore, "The Adolescent Brain," *Edge*, June 5, 2012.

49   Sarah-Jayne Blakemore.

50   Jason Chein et al, "Peers Increase Adolescent Risk Taking by Enhancing Activity in the Brain's Reward Circuitry," *Developmental Science*, vol. 14:2, 2011.

51   Jason Chein et al.

52   Jason Chein et al.

53   Li-Hui Chen et al, "Carrying Passengers as a Risk Factor for Crashes Fatal to 16- and 17-year-old Drivers," *Journal of the American Medical Association*, vol. 283:12, 2000.

54   Marie Claude Ouimet et al, "Young Drivers and Their Passengers: A Systematic Review of Epidemiological Studies on Crash Risk. *Journal of Adolescent Health*, vol. 57, 2015.

55   Marie Claude Ouimet.

56   Marie Claude Ouimet.

57   Marie Claude Ouimet.

58   Interview with David Strayer.

59   Janet Creaser et al, "Are Cellular Phone Blocking Applications Effective for Novice Teen Drivers?" *Journal of Safety Research*, Vol. 54, 2015.

60   Interview with Nichole Morris, September 29, 2015.

61   Creaser et al.

62   Creaser et al.

63   Creaser et al.

64   Interview with Nichole Morris.

65   Interview with Nichole Morris.

66   www.navdy.com

67   "Navdy Feels Like Driving in the Future," www.youtube.com/watch?v=pKL4PJICS40.

68   Interview with Deborah Hersman, March 26, 2015.

69   Matt Richtel, "Windshield Devices Bring Distracted Driving Debate to Eye Level," *New York Times*, May 29, 2015.

70   Ben D. Sawyer et al, "Google Glass: A Driver Distraction Cause or Cure?" *Human Factors*, November 1, 2014.

71   Chris Ziegler, "Meet the Man Behind CarPlay and Android Auto at GM," October 31, 2015, Theverge.com.

72   Interview with Jake Nelson, August 28, 2015.

73   Interview with Jake Nelson.

74   Bianca Bosker, "Ray LaHood Wants To Completely Disable Drivers' Phones (And Keep Google Glass Off Their Heads)," Huffingtonpost.com, November 11, 2013.

75   Christopher Jensen, "50 Years Ago, 'Unsafe at Any Speed' Shook the Auto World," *New York Times*, November 26, 2015.

76   Governors Highway Safety Association, "Seat Belt Laws," February 2016, ghsa.org.

77   Governors Highway Safety Association, 2016.

78   Governors Highway Safety Association, 2016.

79   National Highway Traffic Safety Administration, "Traffic Safety Facts, 2008 Data," www-nrd.nhtsa.dot.gov/Pubs/811160.pdf.

80   Maria Wilhelm, "A Grieving, Angry Mother Charges That Drunken Drivers Are Getting Away with Murder," *People*, June 29, 1981.

81   David J. Hansen, "Candy Lightner: Founder of MADD," alcoholproblemsandsolutions.org.

82   "The History of MADD," madd.org.

83   Email interview with Senator Amy Klobuchar, August 27, 2015.

84   Email interview with Senator Amy Klobuchar.

85   "Distracted Driving," Insurance Institute for Highway Safety, iihs.org.

86   Minnesota Statute § 169.13, Subd. 2.: "Careless driving. Any person who operates or halts any vehicle upon any street or highway carelessly or heedlessly in disregard of the rights of others, or in a manner that endangers or is likely to endanger any property or any person, including the driver or passengers of the vehicle, is guilty of a misdemeanor."

87   Minnesota Statute §§ 609.2112 (death) and 609.2113 (injury)

88   Interview with Robert Speeter, February 15, 2016.

89   Interview with Robert Speeter.

90   "Updated: Texting Minnetonka Driver Charged with Hitting Woman in Crosswalk," *Sun Sailor*, October 22, 2013.

91   Hennepin County Fourth Judicial District Court sentencing document filed June 1, 2015.

92   Interview with Robert Speeter, February 15, 2016.

93   Interview with Tiffani Schweigart, September 15, 2015

94   Interview with Tiffani Schweigart

95   Bill Hudson, "Charges: Girl, 17, Was On Facebook Seconds Before Double Fatal Crashm" CBS Minnesota, minnesota.cbslocal.com, Oct. 19, 2015

96   Interview with Col. Matthew Langer, October 6, 2015.

97   Interview with Col. Matthew Langer.

98   Interview with Col. Matthew Langer.

99   Interview with Col. Matthew Langer.

100   "Minnesota Graduated Driver Licensing,"
       graduateddriverlicensing.com.

101   Interview with Nancy Johnson, May 4, 2015.

102   Interview with Nancy Johnson.

103   Interview with Gordy Pehrson (focus group), September 15,
       2015.

104   Nancy Johnson, "Our Stories: Tina Johnson," Minnesotans for
       Safe Driving, mnsafedriving.com.

105   Interview with Nancy Johnson.

106   Interview with Frank Douma (focus group), September 15,
       2015.

107   "Distracted Driving," Minnesota Office of Traffic Safety, 2016.

108   Interview with Gordy Pehrson (focus group).

109   Interview with Paul Aasen (focus group), September 15, 2015.

110   Jacob Gershman, "Senders of Texts to Drivers Can Be Held
       Liable, Court Rules," *Wall Street Journal,* August 27, 2013.

111   Jacob Gershman.

112   Interview with Arthur Kosieradzki, August 13, 2015.

113   Interview with Robert Speeter.

114   Interview with Senator Amy Klobuchar.

115   "Chevrolet MyLink," www.chevrolet.com/2014-mylink-radio.
       html

116   Ecker et al, "Correcting False Information in Memory:
       Manipulating the Strength of Misinformation Encoding and
       its Retraction," *Psychonomic Bulletin & Review,* vol. 18, June
       2011.

117   Ecker et al.

118   Interview with Ray LaHood, May 20, 2015.

119   Interview with Ray LaHood.

120   Secretary Ray LaHood Distracted Driving Press Conference,
       U.S. Department of Transportation, January 20, 2011, www.
       transportation.gov.

121 "Distracted Driving Campaign," U.S. Department of Transportation, October 26, 2015, www.transportation.gov.

122 Interview with Ray LaHood.

123 Bianca Bosker, "Ray LaHood Wants To Completely Disable Drivers' Phones (And Keep Google Glass Off Their Heads)," Huffingtonpost.com, November 11, 2013.

124 Interview with Donna Berger, November 19, 2015.

125 Interview with Donna Berger.

126 Interview with Ramona Dohman, October 6, 2015.

127 Interview with Ramona Dohman.

128 National Safety Council, "Employer Ban Cell Phone Policy: A Case Study," 2014, www.nsc.org

129 Interview with Paul Aasen, September 1, 2015.

130 Interview with Paul Aasen.

131 Interview with Paul Aasen.

132 Interview with Jennifer Zamora-Jameson, August 1, 2015.

133 Interview with Jennifer Zamora-Jameson.

134 Interview with Jennifer Zamora-Jameson.

135 Interview with Jennifer Zamora-Jameson.

136 Interview with Joel Feldman, November 24, 2015.

137 Interview with Joel Feldman.

138 Interview with Jon Cummings, November 30, 2015.

139 Interview with Jon Cummings.

140 Sarah-Jayne Blakemore, "The Adolescent Brain," *Edge*, June 5, 2012.

141 Sarah-Jayne Blakemore.

142 Simon Sinek, Start with Why: How Great Leaders Inspire Everyone to Take Action, Penguin, 2009.

143 Interview with Matt Richtel, October 22, 2015.

144 Interview with Matt Richtel.

145   Anupreeta Das and Leslie Scism, "Car Crashes are on the Rise, and Warren Buffet Blames Texting," *Wall Street Journal,* September 9, 2015, www.wsj.com/articles/car-crashes-are-on-the-rise-and-warren-buffett-blames-texting-1441800119

146   "Navdy's HUD Feels Like Driving in the Future," navdy.com, August 5, 2014, blog.navdy.com/navdys-hud-feels-like-driving-in-the-future/

147   "U.S. DOT Releases Guidelines to Minimize In-Vehicle Distractions," NHTSA.gov, April 23, 2013

148   Lindsey Seavert, "Texting and Driving: Message Still Not Received," KARE11, www.kare11.com/story/traffic/2015/11/16/texting-and-driving-on-minnesota-roads-a-message-still-not-received/75907774/

Made in the USA
Middletown, DE
10 September 2016